Sylvia Abrego-Araiza

Richard Rittmaster

EMS

Jerry Leener

Catherine Silverman

Barbara Chandler Allen

Kirk Rademaker

Betsy McCarthy

Also by Jane Pauley

Skywriting: A Life Out of the Blue

YOUR LIFE CALLING

Reimagining the Rest of Your Life

JANE PAULEY

Simon & Schuster

New York   London   Toronto   Sydney   New Delhi

90

Simon & Schuster
1230 Avenue of the Americas
New York, NY 10020

First Simon & Schuster hardcover edition January 2014

SIMON & SCHUSTER and colophon are registered trademarks of Simon & Schuster, Inc.

For information about special discounts for bulk purchases, please contact Simon & Schuster Special Sales at 1-866-506-1949 or business@simonandschuster.com.

The Simon & Schuster Speakers Bureau can bring authors to your live event. For more information or to book an event, contact the Simon & Schuster Speakers Bureau at 1-866-248-3049 or visit our website at www.simonspeakers.com.

Interior design by Nancy Singer
Jacket photograph by Kelly Campbell
Endpaper photo credits are on page 253.

Manufactured in the United States of America

10 9 8 7 6 5 4 3 2 1

Library of Congress Cataloging-in-Publication Data
Pauley, Jane.
   Your life calling : reimagining the rest of your life / Jane Pauley.
      pages cm
   1. Career changes—Case studies. 2. Change (Psychology)
3. Self-realization. 4. Middle-aged persons—Psychology. 5.
Pauley, Jane, 1950–
   I. Title.
   HF5384.P38 2014
   650.1—dc23
   2013033711

ISBN 978-1-4767-3376-0
ISBN 978-1-4767-3379-1 (ebook)

In memory of my mother and father,

Richard and Mary Pauley

Contents

Introduction Moment of Impact   xi

Chapter One Out of the Blue   1

Chapter Two The Holy Grail   11

Chapter Three Something More   21

Chapter Four Do-Overs   29

Chapter Five Changes   39

Chapter Six Daughter of a Musician   49

Chapter Seven The Gift   53

Chapter Eight The Next Act   69

Chapter Nine Finding Balance   75

Chapter Ten In Alignment   83

Chapter Eleven Packing for a Long Trip   91

Chapter Twelve "And She Landed on Her Feet"   99

Contents

Chapter Thirteen Up Periscope   107

Chapter Fourteen Less THINK, More DO   115

Chapter Fifteen Inspiration Is Everywhere   123

Chapter Sixteen Work You Want to Do   131

Chapter Seventeen The Mother of Reinvention   135

Chapter Eighteen Epiphanies Happen   147

Chapter Nineteen One Step at a Time   157

Chapter Twenty Spirit of Adventure   169

Chapter Twenty-one Do Something Different   177

Chapter Twenty-two Two Degrees of Cooperation   187

Chapter Twenty-three Back to School   197

Chapter Twenty-four The Call of the Wild   207

Chapter Twenty-five Reality Checks   215

Chapter Twenty-six Talk Therapy   225

Chapter Twenty-seven Just Say Yes   231

Chapter Twenty-eight Commencement   237

Acknowledgments   245

YOUR
LIFE
CALLING

Introduction: Moment of Impact

My friend Meg was successfully treated for thyroid cancer in her thirties, but for the next ten years she faced every annual checkup braced for bad news. When she arrived for lunch after her latest visit to the doctor, she was wearing such a worried expression we were prepared for the worst. But here's what her doctor had said: "Meg, I think you've dodged a bullet. I don't think that cancer is coming back." Good news! And yet the look on her face was not joy or even relief.

I think Meg had been living year to year. Now, suddenly facing the prospect that she might go on living a long time, she felt completely unprepared. This is what she said: "What am I going to *do* for forty years?"

It's the question of the age—and the question of *our* age. My generation is the first to get a heads-up that, as one expert puts it, "our working lives could well be exceeded by the years we go on living." But what *are* we going to *do*? The demographics of aging have been improving, adding decades to what we commonly know as "midlife," but as Laura Carstensen, Ph.D., director of the Stanford Center on Longevity, says, "The culture hasn't had time to catch up. The enormity of this hasn't hit people." It's starting to. At lunch that day with Meg I witnessed a moment of impact.

Everyone is talking about reinvention. The president used the word "reinvention" nine times in a State of the Union address. The *Harvard Business Review* devoted an entire issue to reinvention. Something profound is happening. But as a woman in my AARP online chat room aptly put it, "I'm ready to reinvent myself. Any ideas about what I should reinvent myself into? Nothing is lining up in front of me." It's a common sentiment. I often hear it described as a *yearning* for something "more." It's a feeling I could personally relate to—being ready for something, but a something you can't quite define. Our vocabulary hasn't caught up.

What does midlife mean? It used to be the beginning of a long glide path into retirement, which many of us still eagerly look forward to. As I write, the morning paper reports that 2 million of us will be retiring in the coming year. Maybe you will be one of those newly minted "retirees." But since you are reading this book, you've probably decided your retirement will be different. Unlike previous generations, who retired *from* something, my generation hopes to retire *to* something else. Midlife keeps on going and going. Even before the economy went into recession, the majority of baby boomers surveyed by AARP reported they expected to keep on working in retirement, which sounds like a contradiction in terms, but it's not. "Retirement" is a word with new meaning—no longer a door marked EXIT. Think instead of a door that swings on a hinge, moving us forward into something new.

Marc Freedman of Encore.org, which helps people pursue second acts for the greater good, says we've been blessed with a "bonus decade or two or three." We still have options. I have met dozens of people who've already been there and done it in *Your Life Calling* (now *Life Reimagined Today*), the series produced for the *Today* show with my partners at AARP. This is a booming demographic. And the Gen Xers are not far behind—they start turning fifty in 2014.

I've been thinking and talking about reinvention for many years. Born in 1950, I'm on the leading edge of the baby boom, and I've had a peek over the horizon. The future looks pretty good.

Not long ago, two sixty-something women filled a sold-out auditorium at my alma mater, Indiana University (class of '72). The evening was billed as "A Conversation with Meryl Streep." I would be asking the questions. The highlight was when Meryl asked and answered her own question, eliciting a gasp from the audience of 3,500 people:

"When Bette Davis starred in *All About Eve*, a movie about a way-over-the-hill actress, how old do you think she was?"

She paused a moment before she said, "Forty!" Then she let that sink in, and brushing her hair back like she does, said in her offhanded way, "So . . . it's really a different world." It really is.

Midlife is different than it used to be. For many it will be much longer, but demographers don't merely talk about longer life expectancy, they also talk about longer *health* expectancy. People living longer and staying healthy longer is a powerful combination.

And there's more. A few years ago researchers made an unexpected discovery that, around the age of forty, people begin to experience feelings of dissatisfaction and a diminished sense of well-being. They were surprised to find this in men and women, rich and poor and all over the world. But the bigger surprise was the rebound effect. At around the age of fifty, feelings of well-being begin to rise again—and keep on rising, well into the seventies. In the twenty-first century, fifty is the beginning of a new and aspirational time of life.

Richard Luker is a social psychologist sometimes called the father of sports research. He created the influential ESPN Sports Poll twenty years ago. He's probably the foremost expert on how Americans spend their leisure time and money. "People who are now in their fifties are far more vital in their outlook than people in their fifties were even ten years ago," he says. "Just now since

2007 these adults are saying, 'not only do I see a more vigorous life, I'm up for it, I'm game, I want to do more.' Our research is bearing that out in spades."

We have all known inspiring individuals who have defied the stereotypes of aging to lead long, creative, and productive lives, but until now that was perceived as the exception. As I read in *The Washington Post*, "Not long ago, workers in their forties were closer to the end of their careers than the beginning." Today men and women in their forties can reasonably be thinking about beginning a new career, or something new that's not a career. We are the first generation to get a heads-up that not only is there more to come, but maybe even the best of all.

You may be surprised to know that people over fifty-five represent the largest age group of owners of new business start-ups. At an age when our own parents and grandparents expected to wind things down, people are getting a second wind.

The Stanford longevity expert, Laura Carstensen, notes that with our new vitality come some pretty big questions. She says, "Those of us living today have been handed a remarkable gift with no strings attached—an extra thirty years of life for the average person. Now that gift is forcing us to answer a uniquely twenty-first-century question—what are we going to do with our supersized lives?"

I don't fashion myself an authority, though as a journalist and storyteller I have long recognized the power of other people's stories to help us to see our own lives in new ways. *Your Life*

Calling: Reimagining the Rest of Your Life is neither a "must do" nor a "how to." But I do hope to challenge some misconceptions you may have about reinvention:

- That you have to get it right the *first time*
- That there is some most authentic "you" waiting to be *revealed*
- That reinvention is a *total makeover*
- That everyone has a *passion* to follow.

I'll endorse a couple of counterintuitive ideas:

- Trial and error are keys to growth and self-knowledge.
- Reinvention may require being reintroduced to yourself.
- Self-discovery may not be the requirement for reinvention but the payoff.

So, this book is filled with stories and not much advice, but I hope you'll find ideas and inspiration in abundance. Perhaps one story will speak to a yearning or discontent you may be familiar with; another may help focus your rising sense of optimism and well-being. Maybe you'll be energized to take a bold first step, or decide to take a step back and reflect.

There will be times when you should pause and listen. The future will be longer than you think. And yet the future is probably closer than you expect. Contradictions abound! It's been my personal observation that if there's a secret to reinvention, it's that there *isn't* one, or rather, there isn't only *one*. There are as many ways to do it as there are experts eager to guide us. As Bertolt Brecht put it, "The shortest line between two points can be a crooked line." For the lucky few, here's a chance to reach toward a long-nurtured dream. For many, the way forward may feel like groping in the dark, as it did for me. Frankly, we are all making it up as we go along. But how reassuring to know we're all in this together.

Chapter One

Out of the Blue

I've been one of the luckiest people I know. Through most of my life good things happened to me. Without a journalism degree, a network of connections, or driving personal ambition—and with very little experience—I landed one of the most coveted jobs in America in 1976. I was Barbara Walters's successor on *Today*. I was very well paid. I enjoyed manageable fame but suffered a gnawing sense that it was somehow illegitimate. I wasn't the only one.

In 1979, David Letterman and I were invited to an event in our hometown, Indianapolis, and I'll never forget how he described *his* television career. He said, "It's like robbing 7-Elevens. The money's good, but sooner or later you know you're gonna get caught." This was a perfect depiction of a popular psychological term—that wouldn't be coined for another two years—"impostor syndrome." There was a lot of that going around.

Paul Giannone had a good job in information technology. But he told me that for twenty years he "masqueraded as a computer nerd."

He explained, "I'm not a geek, but I chose a job where I had to appear to be one." When I pointed out that he seemed to have succeeded, he replied, "Well, you can grind it out. You ever see somebody who doesn't have that music gene play a piano? They could get it done, but they're not going to be at Carnegie Hall any time soon."

Here is a very smart guy. But in information technology everyone is smart, smarter, or *wicked* smart. He said he couldn't sleep the night before a presentation to his so-called peers. He suffered cold sweats. Every business presentation was another opportunity to measure himself against everyone in the audience. And by his own estimation, he inevitably came up short.

As he was telling me this story, I was trying to picture this guy with stage fright. He was such an extrovert I had to ask how with his personality he had ever majored in accounting. He said, "I got A's in math."

It's a truism that most of us don't really choose our careers as much as we "fall into" them:

"It was my first job out of college, and then I got a promotion . . ."

"My husband was transferred here, so I got a job, too . . ."

"In my family, we're all doctors."

You've got to have the goods to get that promotion, to get through medical school, to be the successful job applicant. But a successful career isn't necessarily a happy one. And a proficiency is not the same as a passion.

Writing in *The New York Times Magazine*, John Jeremiah Sullivan recounted a cushy-sounding reporting assignment to "get lots of massages." Between massages, he mused that massage was "one of those jobs you fall into when other things don't work out. But that's true for so many of us—we fall into our lines of work like coins dropping into slots, bouncing down off various failures and false starts."

My career in television felt like that—a coin dropping into a slot—though instead of bouncing off failures and false starts, I won the jackpot. In the course of a single year, I went from the anchor desk of WISH-TV's "The Big News" in Indianapolis (the *weekend* edition), to become the first woman to anchor the evening news in Chicago. And I was only twenty-four.

A year later on *Today*, when *TV Guide* pronounced me "the fastest rising personality in the history of television," my more seasoned partner, Tom Brokaw, joked that I sounded like a "brown and serve roll." My career was most distinguished by its trajectory, and its velocity was inexplicable. I tried in vain to explain it to myself. Especially in light of some memorable and less than flattering reviews in Chicago. *The Chicago Daily News* compared me to a "hood ornament." *The Chicago Tribune* reported I had "the IQ of a cantaloupe." The local media had a lot of fun at my expense, and it was a given that I was not long for Chicago. To be honest, I thought they were right. And they were. But I was as stunned as everyone else when I was soon packing my bags—for New York. There was just no explaining it!

I would often think of *The Sound of Music*, in which a very young Maria struggled to explain her unexpected good fortune. She had found love—rather, love had found her in the handsome Captain von Trapp, who sent a glamorous fiancée packing to propose marriage to the new nanny. Dizzy with disbelief, our lucky heroine sang herself to a happy and logical conclusion—that in her childhood she must have done "something good" to deserve it.

I took an entirely different view of my good luck. As Tom Brokaw told *The Washington Post* back when we were getting to know each other on *Today*, "Jane is very realistic about her deficiencies." I think I kept myself grounded by advertising them. My introductory words on *Today* were, "Maybe you're wondering how I got here. Maybe I am, too!"

In 1976, network anchors weren't just smarter, they were older. My putative peers included veteran newsmen like Walter Cronkite. Tom Brokaw was a boyish-looking thirty-something up-and-comer himself, but Tom was born with gravitas. The qualities audiences looked for in journalism back then—that *I* looked for in network newsmen and women—were maturity and seasoning. What I lacked in seasoning, I suppose I made up for in *freshness*.

I think my most singular accomplishment as a network anchor not very long out of college was appearing to keep my head on straight while it was spinning. But I wasn't faking it. My husband likes to tell the story about the morning I did a run-through before the show of a segment about testing blood pressure. Later, when I did the segment live, my blood pressure had *fallen*. In audience research (which I didn't see until decades later), I consistently got high marks for authenticity. And perhaps in a nation weary after decades of civil rights struggle, Vietnam, and Watergate, freshness and authenticity were not to be underrated. But that's the perspective of hindsight. I was so young, and every day was an opportunity to measure myself against my esteemed peers, and to come up short. Just like Paul Giannone.

Paul's proficiency in math led him first to accounting, but back in the early 1980s he made a shrewd transition into the new field of information technology. Not only was everyone smart but every year they were smarter and younger.

When he was offered a buyout in his forties, Paul grabbed it. He looked forward to being his own boss. But he quickly discovered that finding freelance work was hard. He went long stretches with no work or work that kept him on the road and away from home. The turning point came after one of those dry spells, when he found work in Texas. Then 9/11 happened. With his family in New Jersey and traumatized by the attack, Paul could not get home. Planes were grounded. A rental car company generously offered to waive the drop-off fee if he drove to New Jersey, but the bottom line was that he had a family to support; he *needed* that job. He felt trapped.

I did too. Though I'd been blessed with more success than I would have imagined in my wildest dreams (had I been a "wildest dreams" sort of person), when I packed a suitcase for some glamorous destination—London, Rio, Rome, China—I was leaving three small children at home. You've heard the phrase "the trappings of success." I looked up the meaning of "trapping": "an ornamental covering or harness for a horse." There came a time when what I most yearned for was *less*.

Careers are abstractions. But we live in them either in harmony or in discord because paychecks and bills and contracts are real. A well-matched career can nourish the spirit, but a mismatched career can enervate the soul. That's when you may feel there must be *more*.

Underneath his angst, Paul Giannone had real passions. He loved to cook. And entertain. For years, friends had been telling him to open a restaurant. He'd say, "You're out of your mind." But then he had his "pizza epiphany." He and his sons had a tradition of making "pizza tours." One of these excursions took them to a place in Coney Island where he had pizza like no pizza he'd had before. A coal-fired oven—that's what made the difference. He started researching pizza ovens. He decided to build one in his own backyard and started telling people he was opening a pizzeria as soon as he bought the bricks. Why? He answered slyly, "Because commitment is a powerful thing."

He told me, "I knew that first I had to prove to myself that

I could even make pizza, and then I would need to practice and experiment. So I didn't build the oven for a hobby. I built it with that goal in mind."

He started building his backyard pizza oven in September 2007. In November, his son called home from the Air Force Academy in Colorado and asked how the oven was coming. Paul said it was coming along, but slowly, because he could work on it only on weekends.

His son said, "Dad, you gotta build that oven. You can't be telling people you're gonna do something and not do it. I'm coming home with my friend for Thanksgiving, and you'd better make me some pizza out of that oven."

"My son loves the chase of my dream," Paul said. "He threw down the challenge. And I knew that both my sons had to see that when you chase your dream, you have to achieve it. If they saw that I just threw it aside, they would think that maybe they were made out of the same stock and they'd throw things aside in their lives, too. So I was propelled by that. And son of a gun, Thanksgiving Eve, we pulled our first pizza out of that oven. It was ridiculous. It looked like an amoeba. But it tasted pretty good. I was just amazed. I had never made pizza before, ever."

"Wait a minute," I said. "You had decided to open a pizzeria and you had never made a pizza?"

"That's correct," he replied.

Where, I wondered, did that confidence come from? Paul shrugged off the difficulty. "You know what," he said, "I looked around and I saw other people had done it and I said if they could do it, so can I."

No longer an impostor, Paul believed pizza making was not only something he could do but something he could excel at. And he deliberately set the bar high. He set out to meet and befriend all of the great pizzaioli in New York. He explained, "I made a real point of looking each of them in the eye and saying, 'It's my hope to be mentioned in the same breath with you one day.' I wasn't afraid to say that. I just knew by verbalizing it I would help make it happen." He added, "You only need two things to succeed: belief and commitment."

Still, one would think that opening a restaurant during a recession might give one pause. Not him. He knew his clientele. "People in New York, they gotta have the best of everything. They hunt it out. But they can't afford to go and hunt out the best steaks all the time. Maybe they could go to Peter Luger's for their birthday once a year, or maybe they could go to a high-end sushi place once in a while. But with pizza, for fifteen dollars or so you could get maybe the best meal in New York. So it was a great time to open up a pizzeria. I asked other pizzaioli how their business was, and they said, 'Better than ever.'"

Paul took the process one step at a time, until he was ready to scout locations. He fell in love with the young hipster energy of Greenpoint, Brooklyn, and then he fell in love with a building. He'd mortgaged his own home to the hilt, but he needed a lot more cash. He was touched that people were interested in investing in him, but I think he pulled it off with the force of his personality and some amazing pies.

Lucky is the person who finds such a perfect fit, though it sometimes comes with a wistfulness about not having discovered it earlier. Paul put it this way: "I just thought that you go out, you pick a career, you work, eventually you build up a retirement fund, you retire, and you go do something you like. I wish they had told me that you need to find something that you like and do it right now for the rest of your life, because that's what everybody should do—find your passion and do it because you're gonna be good at it."

Sometimes it takes the better part of a lifetime to find out what your passion is, but in my observation, if you do, it might be the best part of your life.

Chapter Two

The Holy Grail

B etsy McCarthy was my first *Your Life Calling* story to air on *Today*, early in 2010. Frankly, I thought it pretty bold to lead off the series with a story about a woman whose reinvention was knitting. One pictures a gray-haired lady in a rocking chair. But Betsy knits like it was an Olympic sport; throughout our interview her fingers were working three tiny needles. And everything she said held our predominantly male crew absolutely rapt. We were all thinking, "I'll have what she's having." Betsy had found the Holy Grail of reinvention. She turned a passionate pastime into a full-time occupation.

Betsy had been a successful executive in the health-care industry. She earned a six-figure salary and enjoyed the respect of her peers, but as she approached fifty, she felt there was just something missing in her life. "I'd get up, go to work, and I'd give it my all. But I started to be aware that I wasn't waking up in the morning and saying, 'Wow! I can't wait to get to that meeting.' Something was bypassing me." She carried a briefcase to work every day. There was always knitting in it. She said it kept her sane.

For Betsy knitting is not a hobby. It's a passion. And as she rose into the executive echelons, with the accompanying high-level stress, knitting was a salve. "I'd get up at five and go into the kitchen with my knitting, and just sort of calm myself as the sun was coming up," she said. "I tried to start my day out in a quiet, centered place, and then I'd get ready for work."

When she had knitting needles in her hands, she felt calmer inside. "It's sort of like Zen or yoga or meditation . . . it's almost comforting," she told me, "like being rocked or like riding a train when I was little, and you'd hear the clacking of the rails. I always looked forward to trains—anything that would make me stop or slow down." She would even knit in the car while waiting for a traffic light to change.

Betsy draws satisfaction from being good at difficult things, and she found the challenge of her job and being respected by her colleagues very rewarding. "Helping a team accomplish more than they thought they could" was a particular source of pride. But work was work. And Betsy had been working all her life. She worked her way through college and graduate school, and had reinvented herself more than once. She started out as an English teacher before switching to budget and policy analysis.

Betsy began taking knitting classes for pleasure, and had the persistent thought that she could be teaching them. While she yearned to leave the nine-to-five world and do something with knitting, colleagues and friends would say, "You're not even fifty. What's going to become of you?" Or, "You're committing career suicide." And then she was recruited for another, better-paying job. But when she was fifty-seven, Betsy finally ditched the briefcase.

On her final day of work, her husband asked, "How does it feel to be getting the last paycheck you're ever going to have?"

"This isn't the last paycheck I'm ever going to have," she replied. Though she hadn't figured out how, she was confident she could make knitting work.

I'm not a hobby person. It was a source of embarrassment in those early days at NBC, when after a morning of interviewing people on *Today*, there was often a reporter in my office waiting to interview *me*. The question I most dreaded was about what I did in my spare time. "Reading and shopping," I told one reporter. Seriously.

But I grew up with people who had all sorts of outside interests. Everyone in my family enjoyed doing things. My father kept his tools in the garage—which he built. My mother was a gifted seamstress. She preferred Vogue patterns, the kind with fifty-two pieces. The hum of her sewing machine meant my mother was happily at work on a project. She made most of our clothes back when making clothes was cheaper than buying them ready-made.

My father wasn't a coin collector, but he counted pennies. He made not spending money look recreational. Numbers were a special category of interest for him. I wouldn't be surprised if he'd made note of exactly how many nails he hammered while building that garage. When he put in the patio in front of our new house, he could tell you how many bags of sand he poured to fill in the cracks between the stones he laid. It made him happy to come back from a walk on the beach during a Florida vacation and report how many steps he took.

These weren't hobbies per se, but my parents cultivated many competencies and outside interests. And so does my husband. In the winter, Garry enjoys gardening catalog reveries. And one day recently when he told me, "I think I've lost the capacity for boredom," I started taking notes.

He explained, "Whenever I'm in a situation I find uninteresting, I simply retreat to the amusement park that is my brain." I already knew Garry had a rich daydream life, including sometimes imagining himself as President of the United States. But he surprised me when he said, "I'm also in a rock band." We were in the car at the time, and just then a song came on the radio. "Hear that?" Garry said. "I'm playing bass." After thirty years of marriage, I'm still making discoveries about his range of interests. Who knew he could play "When the Saints Go Marching In" on a one-and-a-half-inch harmonica!

Garry didn't waste a moment of his childhood, and along with a rich imagination, he cultivated competencies. He's an artist, for example, who's pretty handy with tools. He built a tree house for the kids—with double-hung windows. If Garry should live another forty years, and I certainly hope he does, he'll make it an interesting journey.

Then there's my sister, Ann. Her long list of outside interests just gets longer. She built a harpsichord from a kit in her twenties. In her thirties she had a Skilsaw and knew how to use it. When she was in her forties there was a loom the size of a small car in her bedroom. Currently, she takes piano lessons as well as photography and drawing classes. I may have married my sister.

Where was I when these genes were passed around? That "what do you do in your spare time" question is still a popular one. Preparing to moderate a panel discussion recently, I Googled one of the panelists. He had a succinct response to the question: "Sleep, ski, sail, repeat." He sounded like a pretty cool dude.

Interesting people do interesting things, so over the years I've tried to cultivate some outside interests. In my late thirties I began dabbling in watercolors. Garry is the artist in the family, and like a kindergartner looking for approval, I remember showing him one of my early efforts and waiting while he studied it for a rather long time, looking for something positive to say. Finally he said, "Well, you know when to stop."

The week after I left the *Today* show, in 1989, I signed up for skating lessons at the famous rink at Rockefeller Center. Signing up for lessons was so not "me," though it was not without precedent. The breakthrough had been knitting lessons in the early eighties. It was as if a nascent creative impulse was trying to break through. I enjoyed those six weekly lessons. They were held on Tuesday nights in a knitting shop, with half a dozen other beginners. We made tiny mouse-sized sweaters. I was immediately inspired to make a much larger version for my husband. It turned out much larger than my husband. We remember it fondly as the "clown sweater." After that I started a baby bunting with decorative little balls, which was pretty ambitious for a beginner. I was pregnant, so it was a race against time. Not only did the baby come first but there were two of them. So the knitting was put away.

Betsy McCarthy was ahead of her time when she quit her job. "Reinvention" wasn't the buzzword it is today. At first, she said, the freedom was very exciting. "I can do whatever I want and there's this whole day ahead of me." But after a while she thought, "Well, this seems like a vacation, but I can't do this for the next forty years."

Her husband would come home from his busy life and ask, "Well, what'd you accomplish today?" She didn't really have an answer, except to say, "That's not the right question." But it took time to find the right answer.

Betsy says uncertainty is something she's always been comfortable with, but she recognizes that if someone needs certainty—"If I do *this*, then *that* will happen tomorrow"—it would be harder for that person to make a leap of faith into a new life. Betsy made the leap *before* she could see her new life. There was a period she described as "a lot of floundering around."

She might have opened her own knitting shop. But she rejected that idea out of hand. Knitting was her passion; running a business was not. Still, she applied some business sense to her new life plan. She explained, "It's like developing a little marketing plan for yourself. You just go out and create the opportunity you want."

She started teaching on cruise ships, and because she has a gift for design, she was hired to write a chapter in a book about knitting Christmas stockings. One day she offhandedly asked the editor, "Are you going to have a book on socks?" The editor said, "Well, why don't you write it?"

So Betsy had a book contract, and *Knit Socks!* is in its sixth printing. While it's made Betsy something like a rock star at knitting conferences, it hasn't made her rich. She makes a four-figure salary—the low four figures. But Betsy had already reevaluated the connection between money and self-worth. Once before when she'd had to look for a new job, she wouldn't consider anything that didn't pay what she thought she was worth, because taking anything less was "devaluing" herself. "But," she said, "I got over thinking that money was how I needed to measure whether life was good to me."

She and her husband did prepare for the financial adjustment. The children were grown, so they downsized. Paying off a mortgage and selling a big house filled with antiques, they moved to a small condo that Betsy described as having lot of built-ins, "sort of like a boat."

"Life is wonderful," she said. "And yarn doesn't cost very much."

Betsy found what had been missing in her life: contentment and satisfaction. She regards her decision to leave the high-powered work world and do something with knitting not as an extreme makeover but as a return to her "essential self," remembering the little girl who was happy making doll dresses and doing creative things with fabric and color, and making things with her hands.

She ran into a former associate a while ago. "In a tone that sounded as if he felt embarrassed or sorry for me, he said, 'I understand you're doing a lot of knitting.' I think he was being protective of me, and he was worried," she said. "But I wasn't. Some people are uncomfortable going into that gray zone, of not knowing exactly what they're moving toward. But at that point in my life, I had learned that if you're open to something, you can find it."

Betsy inspired me to get out my knitting needles again. Every several years they call to me, but I never progress beyond beginner. Still, I find it very calming—knitting one way and purling back.

Everyone asks a knitter, "What are you making?"

I just say, "Rows."

Chapter Three

Something More

When I appeared on *Today* in 1976, I don't recall any particular notice paid to the arrival of the first baby boomer at a network news anchor desk. My generation had already upended popular culture, conspired to end a war, and helped to end a presidency, but we thought we'd be forever young—while everyone who *wasn't* us thought we'd never grow up. As the first wave of boomers entered the labor market, our impact was phenomenal, but not boomer-specific. It bolstered and amplified the second great civil rights movement, which was the women's movement. Broadcast journalism was becoming a very popular college major, especially for women, who for the first time were graduating at higher rates than men. Young women were turning up on anchor desks in cities and towns everywhere. And Americans were becoming accustomed to coed anchor teams.

In a segment on the *Today* show after Geraldine Ferraro's vice presidential nomination, in 1984, the political analyst Sidney Blumenthal credited the historic presence of a woman on the presidential ticket to the fact that Americans had seen this before. "We see all the time, a man and a woman on television, interpreting the world to us, and we see them with credibility. This [Mondale-Ferraro] is America's anchor team."

I landed my first job in television in the fall of 1972. Lee Giles, the news director at WISH-TV, in Indianapolis, says before he hired me he'd never even interviewed anyone without a degree in journalism or any journalism experience, if not both. I had neither. Years later, when I was inducted as a fellow of the Society of Professional Journalists, Lee was invited to introduce me, and he quickly sought to dispel a notion long perpetuated by me, that I owed my career to *luck*. "Give me a break, Jane!" He wanted some credit for his perspicacity. He also mentioned, to my great surprise, that two hundred women had applied for the job. But the fact remains, I was lucky to be applying for the job when women were getting interviews. In the spring of 1972, the FCC added two words to an affirmative action clause pertaining to TV licensing—"and women." Perhaps as a result, local TV was far ahead of the networks in putting women on camera. As a "leading-edge" baby boomer, not only was I at the head of the line but I arrived in the labor market at a time of growth and prosperity. Following the sixties "youthquake," the 1970s was the decade of the working woman. And with a certain inevitability, the 1980s was the decade of the working mother. I hit the trifecta.

When I started a family in the 1980s, as millions of us did, I happened to be one of the two most visible working mothers in America. The television pioneer Fred Friendly reportedly said, "Two women made a difference in helping the public understand that pregnancy was a 'condition,' not an 'illness.'" If so, it was likely the only time my name was used in the same sentence with Lucille Ball's.

When her pregnancy was written into the *I Love Lucy* script in the 1950s, it was utterly unprecedented. A generation later, I was pregnant on camera five days a week. Though the historical record should show that Joan Lunden, my counterpart on *Good Morning America*, actually started our baby boom, I trumped her first pregnancy with twins. One or the other of us was pregnant for most of the eighties.

It was a novelty that made news. When my twins were born, a wire story reported that the boy would be called Richard (Ross's first name) and the girl *Twinba*. My daughter, Rachel (who we'd call Rickie), had arrived in the world minutes after her brother and must have been identified in some hospital record as "Twin B." A colleague sent me a copy of the wire story, appending a note that he'd been rooting for Trixie.

My *Today* partners, Tom Brokaw and later Bryant Gumbel, had children too, but working fathers were not news. Working mothers were. We were charting a new course. We were the first generation of women to have so many choices. We could choose to marry or not. We could choose careers or choose full-time motherhood. This was the apogee of "having it all," and that mythical superwoman who seemed able to *do* it all. The counterpoint to all our choices was the reality that "all of the above" was never an option. Working-mother angst was epidemic, and I was not immune. Every morning I left three small children at home. (Tom had arrived two and a half years after the twins.) I was lucky to leave them in the care of a trained nanny, but I paid for my good fortune in guilt and self-doubt. I'd been raised by a stay-at-home mom who saw me off to school every single morning, and was there to see that I changed into my playclothes every afternoon when I came home.

I was on the air when my children got up in the morning. When they were older, Garry walked them to school, and the nanny welcomed them home. Though I didn't share the details of our family life—Garry and I were very protective of our privacy—I was pretty open about sharing my working-mother angst: if I had a full-time job, that could only mean I was a part-time mother. So much for work-life balance.

My anxiety was compounded by the guilty recognition that I had no right to complain. For *Today* viewers, I was the proxy on a travelogue of exotic locations. I covered royal weddings and broadcast from the Great Wall of China and the Olympics, not to mention half a dozen presidential nominating conventions and inaugurations. *Today* televised a private audience with the Pope. With cameras rolling, His Holiness Pope John Paul II blessed a picture of my twins. I appeared to be the luckiest woman in America and emblematic of "having it all."

Looking back, I wish I'd been a little easier on myself. No generation of mothers ever had it easy. My grandmother was a stay-at-home mom, a.k.a. farmwife. She worked sunup to sundown raising three children—and pigs, chickens, and a garden. Gardening wasn't her hobby. Her garden grew peas and tomatoes and beans—staples for the dinner table. And she watered it by hand, filling a watering can from a hand pump in the driveway. But it was the life she chose.

My grandmother was a turn-of-the-century story of reinvention. She trained as a nurse, graduating in her starched whites in 1906. My grandfather was an accountant when they met. I suspect my grandmother was the alpha figure in that marital equation, because when they "went to housekeeping," as she described it, they pooled their resources and bought a farm. One of my grandfather's ten siblings, a sister, had died of tuberculosis, which was the scourge of the era before penicillin, and to my grandmother's educated mind, the fresh air of the farm was healthier than a dank office environment. Though she was right, I suspect my grandfather might have been happier cultivating rows of numbers than rows of soybeans. But farm they did—though she didn't raise her daughters to be farmwives. She wanted them to have something different, something *more*. There was no end of work to be done on the farm, but my grandmother prioritized homework over chores. The family joke was that my aunt Martha would happily have traded her homework for chores.

The Giacomini sisters were raised with a similar ethos on a dairy farm in Point Reyes, California, where as their father Bob Giacomini told me, "The girls weren't really that interested in cows." Diane, Karen, Lynn, and Jill had been raised by a mother who had also prioritized education. I never had the privilege of meeting their mother, Dean; she died one year before I told their story. One by one the girls went off to school and started careers and families scattered around Northern California. But one day Bob called the girls home. We were sitting around the kitchen table when Diane told me the reason. "It was, what are we going to do with the family farm?" The dairy for decades produced milk. But the milk business was getting tougher and Bob was getting older. Karen recalled, "He started talking about cheese."

I teased him about that. "My theory is that you lured your kittens back home with cheese." He wouldn't admit it, but he couldn't deny it. The evidence speaks for itself. As Lynn said, "My Dad has had this farm for fifty-four years and we want it to be around another fifty-four." The kittens came home and with the support of husbands and brothers-in-law, affectionately known as the "outlaws," all four girls helped Bob reinvent the Giacomini Dairy as they reinvented themselves. Lynn brought her background in the wine industry and knowledge of artisanal food. Jill put her Silicon Valley job on hold at first but finally made the decision, declaring "I'm never going back." She brought her marketing expertise. Karen had been a full-time mom. She does a lot of the cooking in the new Culinary Center, which draws agri-tourism. She hopes her sons will be the fourth generation on Giacomini Dairy. Diane, the eldest, was the last to join. When her twenty-year banking career was stalled by the recession, it was "the best thing that ever happened to me." Diane is now the CFO of Point Reyes Cheese.

They were all "paid in cheese" for the first five years. It was a financial gamble and a lot work, but it's paid off. The other day I saw a salad garnished with Point Reyes blue cheese on the menu of a fancy New York Restaurant.

The story of the Point Reyes Cheese sisters was the thirty-third segment of my *Life Reimagined* series and a record for our team. In three minutes and thirty seconds we managed to tell the story of *five* reinventions. "I've got all four of them back," Bob told me. "I'm the luckiest guy on earth." Several weeks before the story aired, Point Reyes Cheese won two SOFI awards (often described as the Oscars for food) in New York City. Bob dedicated the awards to his wife, Dean.

My generation was lucky. We were the first to have choices. It was great, but it was complicated. When my friend Meg retired from her legal career to be a stay-at-home mother of three, she pronounced herself "guilty." I was a working mother of three and arrived at the same verdict. We commiserated regularly. And I had a platform to talk about our universal angst—a kind of talk therapy. Women's magazines were filled with advice about "the balancing act" and "juggling," and I was regularly interviewed. I made a point, given the chance, to be a "having it all" debunker. Women often quote me back to myself even now: "What 'having it all' means to me is guilt, burnout, and stress!" Or, "Career, family, social life—pick two." Or, "You can have it all. Just not all at the same time." Young women are still talking about the balancing act today, but these days young men are too. According to the Pew Research Center, as gender roles converge, men are also becoming concerned about work-family balance. A 2013 Pew survey shows that 56 percent of working moms and 50 percent of working dads say they find it very or somewhat difficult to balance these responsibilities.

My friend Katy may have coined the word "kidults" to describe her nearly grown-up children. We never stop being parents, but as our children get older we outgrow our working-parent angst, and may notice we've kept growing too. We have options our mothers and grandmothers never imagined at this new stage of life. While options mean choices, reinvention is not the reincarnation of the "having it all" fantasy. We're older and wiser.

Chapter Four

Do-Overs

I was invited to a conference at my alma mater and was put up at the IU student union, which hadn't changed at all. I half expected to see a long-haired Janie come around the corner as I waited to check in. But the young woman at the registration desk was having trouble finding a reservation on her computer. My host seemed embarrassed by the delay, and I thought I heard him say something that sounded like "She's an antique."

The young woman brightened and repeated it: "Antique!"—as if it should have been obvious.

Now even more embarrassed, my host explained the special distinction of being assigned a guest room in the antique *wing*.

After I settled in, I called Garry to share the story, saying I supposed that meant the furniture in my room was even older than I was, but he pointed out that in some states "the legal threshold for an antique is sixty years." I'd just turned sixty.

Garry feels safe making little jokes along those lines, because he knows that I know he's under the illusion that his wife still looks great. He's not delusional. His doctor says he has cataracts, but it's too soon to fix them.

I have no reservations about talking about getting older. For most of my life I was self-conscious about being too young. When I took to describing myself as "middle-aged" in my late thirties, an NBC executive suggested I "knock it off." But I think it probably started when my parents enrolled me in first grade when I was only five. Academically, I was ready for school, but my social development must have lagged a bit. The only blight on my report card was the N (for "needs improvement") beside "using playtime" in second grade. Who fails recess?

Starting college on the younger side of my freshman cohort, I felt *way* too young. Not realizing that being a freshman was hard for everyone, I told everybody "I'm *only* seventeen"; it was practically my middle name. I was not trying to appear precocious. To the contrary, I think the idea was to *lower* expectations. Fast-forward to the fall of 1976. When I was introduced as the newest and youngest-ever member of the *Today* on-air family to occupy a chair recently vacated by Barbara Walters, my youth and inexperience seemed to have been self-evident. But I wanted it clearly understood that I knew it, too. It wasn't a minute before I confessed to being "*only* twenty-five." I must have brought it up a lot, because one morning Barbara Howar, the indomitable Texas socialite of the Johnson era, was a guest on the show and took me aside for some woman-to-woman advice. "Jane, honey, you've got to stop telling people how old you are. They're gonna remember!"

Barbara had a lot more confidence in my career than I did. Growing old at NBC seemed a pretty unlikely prospect. My contract was written in thirteen-week cycles, hardly a long-term commitment. It was more like we were dating. Over three decades later, I'm *still* telling people how old I am. For the record: I was born on Halloween, 1950.

I've heard that a successful Chinese author, when asked how old she is, will say, "Unless you want to marry me, what difference does it make?" My aunt Martha had the opposite point of view. Late in life, she confessed she looked forward to telling people how old she was because they would look at her in stunned disbelief—until one day they didn't. But she still got the laugh.

If I have a role model, it might be Aunt Martha—her optimism, resilience, stamina, and sense of humor. But I can almost hear her saying, "What's all this fuss about reinvention?" Reinvention was a way of life for her.

A friend of mine remembers as a little girl being asked what she wanted to be when she grew up and answering forthrightly, "A widow!" She might not have had a clear grasp of the concept, but that's what everyone called her grandmother, who was the kind of colorful, independent woman Texans describe as "a hoot." And what little girl wouldn't want to be like that?

My aunt was kind of a hoot, too. And she was also a widow. When my uncle died, she was only fifty and had a son to raise. She just got on with life. Though she lived to be ninety-four, I'm confident it never occurred to Aunt Martha to wonder, "What am I going to do for forty years?"

My aunt was the only working mother I knew in the early 1960s. I remember a series of jobs. First, selling ladies' clothes at one of the better department stores at the mall. Then she got a real-estate license because it offered more independence. Then she worked at a savings and loan for steadier hours, rising to be branch manager. She was robbed one day—I heard the call on the police radio in the newsroom.

At the age of sixty-five, Aunt Martha stuffed her mandatory retirement papers in her purse and walked across the street to a travel agency. She wasn't planning a trip. She got a job as a tour guide. She finally officially retired ten years later, at seventy-five, but that was only because the travel agency closed. And she still had almost twenty years to go. She went on volunteering. When she boasted once about how she got all the "old folks" at the nursing home to sing their high school songs, we wondered if she wasn't older than most of those "old folks." She was a born entertainer. I have no doubt that attendance at her weekly Bible Club was boosted by the understanding that Aunt Martha always got things started with a joke.

. . .

Gid Pool was born a jokester. He didn't really need to be introduced to the concept of reinvention either. "I get bored easily," he told me. Gid was a jack-of-all-trades with a résumé that included seminary student and ski instructor, Army and Air Force. He sold vacuum cleaners door to door. He sold boats, cars, insurance, and real estate. The list goes on and on.

"I was very good at trying things," he told me, not that he was proud of it. When I asked him, "How would you fill in the blank under 'occupation'?" he said, "Road show."

He didn't see it like I did. Being good at "trying things" is why he tried something in his sixties that has utterly changed his life. His career is *literally* a road show now, and he's found more happiness on the road than he could ever have imagined.

When he was sixty-one, Gid went to McCurdy's Comedy Theatre in Sarasota, Florida, to lend support to a friend who had enrolled in a stand-up comedy class, and at graduation had to perform a set in front of a live audience. And he was very funny. Sitting in the audience, laughing, Gid thought, "That looks like fun." He also thought maybe it was something he could do.

"If I can go through the class and just do the show and not embarrass myself and get some laughs, then it would be worth it," he figured. And there was something else: "I didn't have fifty more years to find out what to do with my life." Being good at trying things, Gid signed up for the next class.

He performed at his own graduation and got laughs and dared to think, "What if I could really do this? What if this is the one thing that I can hook myself in to and just see how far I can go and not get sidetracked partway through it?" But a part of him was worried. "I was afraid when I started actually doing it and doing the open mikes that I would do what I've done with everything else—get into it a little bit, get distracted, and go off and do something else." Comedy brought him full circle. Fifty years before, he'd been the "class clown"—the cutup—but deep inside he'd always felt like a bit of a screwup. And those old feelings came back. His lifelong pattern was to jump into things and then lose interest. Would this time be different? Time would tell. Of course, there was another question—was he really any good? The only way to find out was to take his show on the road.

For every minute standing onstage, a comic spends hours honing material and days on the road. For two years Gid worked the comedy club "open mike" circuit. It was grueling. He'd drive for four hours, do a five-minute set, and then turn around and drive four hours home. If he got paid at all, he'd probably spent more on gas.

The venues were often bars. "They'd put a stage at the end of the bar, and a bunch of us would get together and we'd all go up and do our five or six minutes and tell each other how funny we were, and then go drink in the back of the bar, and then come back the next week and do it again." He did some second-guessing, but kept at it. He got better, and, as he got better, he got better gigs in venues like churches and clubs. He started to think, "I can do this."

Hearing him tell this story, I suggested, "You'd finally grown up."

He laughed. "Grew up? Really? I'm a comedian. You can't use 'grown up' and 'comedian' in the same sentence."

Gid is disinclined ever to take himself too seriously. But he does marvel at his change in attitude. As he told me with some degree of wonderment, "I've had jobs where—I won't say I mailed it in, I did okay, but I didn't sit up at night worrying about how well I was doing my job. Now I stay up until one or two o'clock in the morning looking at videos of me onstage, changing things, adding things, to make it better." His wife, Jane, is his biggest fan and best critic. She's in the audience taping every show. He has a computer program to measure the laughs. (Professionals deliver a laugh every eighteen seconds.) Being funny is hard work. And Gid works hard at it. He is focused. He is disciplined.

Would the younger Gid recognize him now?

"No, no. I barely recognize me now."

He calls his style the "grumpy old man." It's working for him. For example, at a recent gig, he noticed two young women in the front row texting on their phones. He asked one of them in a deliberately confused-sounding voice, "Excuse me, is that one of those fancy phones that get the Internet?"

"Yeah," she said, smirking.

"Could you Google 'manners'?"

The audience roared.

Gid thinks part of his secret is just being himself. "I come without wrappings, without a bow around me. I've got dents. I'm the old rusted-out Opel everyone loved when they were growing up." (I could relate. My first car was an Opel. Sad but true story: I actually paid the sticker price. Duh!)

The "class clown" who craved attention is really getting attention. He was featured in *The Wall Street Journal*. I put him on network TV. He never dreamed it could be this way. It's all a little overwhelming, in fact. Gid teared up when he said, "Sometimes I look at all of this, and it's like I feel like I wasted all those years, because I didn't do something big and special with my life. And then I realize that I got this do-over and I get a chance to do something bigger than I thought I could ever do. And it sort of hurts that it took this long, you know. It hurts sometimes that I feel like that there were all of these opportunities that people gave me that I didn't take advantage of."

But Gid feels lucky. "We're the first generation that gets a do-over," he told me. "My grandfather, when he was my age, was beat up physically. He had worked on a railroad all of his life as an engineer. But if my heart goes bad, they'll fix it. If my eyesight goes bad, they'll fix it."

At age sixty-seven, Gid got a do-over. And he's having the time of his life.

• • •

What fascinates me about my *Your Life Calling* stories is tracing people's career paths. The twists and turns lives take are not as random as they might seem. A friend of mine has a résumé his wife describes as a series of "hairpin turns," each one preparing him for a completely logical destination no one would have predicted. Moving forward in life is rarely a straight line; we may even circle back.

The day of my first *Your Life Calling* appearance on *Today*, I got flowers with a card that said, "Congratulations on your return to where it all began." They were from my husband. Coming full circle is very different from going back to square one.

The *Today* show had not stood still in my absence. Back in my day, leaving for work before dawn sometimes defied New York City's reputation as "the city that never sleeps." It was a pretty quiet place. The sound of a floor polisher was the only sign of life at 30 Rock. Up in Studio 3B, Tom Brokaw might be leisurely paging through the morning paper sipping coffee, a low hum of chatter coming from the control room. Today's *Today* runs on jet fuel, not caffeine. The once sleepy greenroom clamors like Times Square.

The more things change, the easier it is to identify what has stayed the same and what is now completely different. Five minutes a month, obviously, is a lot different than five days a week. But if I've returned to *Today* considerably older, I'm also considerably smarter. And I'm not wondering how it happened anymore. This time I made it happen.

Chapter Five

Changes

Looking out upon the bright young women of Radcliffe College, class of '90, I explained, "I was invited to come today, despite the fact that, as my daughter put it this morning, 'You'd rather stay home with your children, wouldn't you?' to talk about women's issues of the nineties and 'having it all.'"

The speech went over pretty well as I recall, though what I remember most vividly is turning from page seven of my text to page nine—with no memory whatever of what I'd written on the missing page eight. I still have the speech—minus page eight—and was surprised to find the word "reinvention" in it.

It's not hard to understand why *I* was thinking about reinvention at the age of thirty-nine. I was still a member of the NBC family that spring but no longer a member of the *Today* family. The story behind my *Today* farewell after thirteen years periodically resurfaces in the churn of more current events. *The New York Times*, May 2013: "A little more than twenty years ago the network replaced Jane Pauley with the younger Deborah Norville; that *Today* show shake-up was so calamitous that it became the founding fiasco of morning television." I'm still asked about those long-ago events. I'm sure Deborah Norville is tired of those questions, too.

To put things in perspective, history will remember 1989 as the year the Iron Curtain fell, but at the time, our behind-the-curtain drama at *Today* competed for attention in the headlines. When Deborah, supersmart, extremely attractive, and ten years *younger*, suddenly appeared on the sofa one morning along with Bryant Gumbel and me, the acerbic and influential *Washington Post* TV critic, Tom Shales, compared the scene to the iconic older woman–younger woman movie, *All About Eve* (the Bette Davis movie Meryl Streep referenced when I interviewed her at Indiana University). That Shales column launched the first media frenzy I'd ever witnessed as a reporter. And I was the center of it. The underlying narrative was that the first baby boomer was being put out to pasture. It was all speculation, because nobody at NBC was talking, except behind closed doors. The media were left to fill in the blanks, and they feasted on this melodrama for weeks until the denouement—my fond, tearful on-air farewell. Last week a woman my age told me she stayed home from work that day to see it.

Twenty-five years later, the author of a book about morning television asked me, "Were you pushed out, or was Deborah pushed in?" I had never heard the situation framed more insightfully. Deborah was pushed in, but I was not pushed out. Though I doubt I would have had the courage to leave without the nudge, I was *asking* to leave.

Given that I interpreted Deborah's presence on the sofa about the same way everyone else had: my replacement had arrived. I was happy to facilitate the transition. I asked to be released from my contract to make way for my successor. I was surprised when NBC's top news executives didn't immediately see the wisdom of my plan. Week after week we talked. There were no tears. There were no threats. But the answer was always no.

Until one day I arrived with an idea—and a new proposal. What if I left *Today* but stayed on at NBC News? Before dawn that morning, as I waited in the lobby of my apartment building for the car that daily delivered me to 30 Rock, I scribbled an outline for a one-hour show. I'd finally faced the fact that NBC News would not let me go. I finally understood that it wasn't about me; it was about my contract. Letting anyone out of a contract was not a precedent NBC was eager to set. But there was a palpable sense of relief in the executive suite later that morning when I explained my idea—a one-hour special about people in transition called *Changes*. It was the way out everyone was looking for. At last I got the answer I wanted—Yes! It was announced that I'd be leaving the *Today* show after Christmas and moving on to other assignments at NBC News.

And at last I was free to speak publicly: "Explaining why I would want to leave the place I've called my second home for most of my adult life . . . the best job in television . . . I'm not completely sure I know. Just that it seemed *time*. Perhaps you know the feeling: 'Is that all there is?' No, I'm not suffering mid-career ennui . . . Turn the question around to catch the light in another way: 'Where do I *go* from here?'"

I had no idea where I was going, but I was eager to hit the road. It's been a recurring theme in my life dating back at least to my sophomore year in college, when I calculated how to earn enough credits to finish a semester early. I was in such a hurry, it was as if I had somewhere to *go*. I did not!

But as Garry said of my watercolor painting, I know when it's time to stop.

So did Jerry Leener. He explained to me, "I went to a base-ball game, and my youngest son hit a home run at the bottom of the seventh inning, and I said, 'I don't ever want to miss another one of these again. I want to be there with my son. I want to be there with my kids.'" Jerry had a highly successful career. He was a partner in a global accounting firm in Maryland. But when he was offered a buyout, he took it.

He felt that same yearning I'd felt—it was time to go. It wasn't the first time. He recalled telling his children's pediatrician, "I want to go to medical school," and the doctor looking at him like he was nuts, saying, "Just stay where you're at. You're making money. You've got a happy family. You don't need this."

But when Jerry was in his mid-fifties, the feeling became more urgent, and the opportunity of a buyout made it irresistible. It was a chance to do something else. But what?

Perhaps because he was an accountant, he took a deliberative approach to reinvention. Among the dozens of people I've profiled, Jerry was the first and so far the only one who embarked on a formal process. Many experts in the books on reinvention that line my shelves at home agree that we all have very individual sets of wants and needs. But they also agree that most of us find it hard to name them.

Perhaps you are familiar with the concept of "flow"—more popularly expressed as being "in the zone." The term was coined by an influential scholar and author whose name I take pride in being able to pronounce: Mihaly Csikszentmihalyi. He says, "Many people can't distinguish between the parts of their work that cause them stress and the parts they actually enjoy."

This likely includes you, and definitely included Jerry Leener and me.

But, with the help of a counselor, Jerry put up a whiteboard and began to identify his "themes," which included making a substantive contribution, having freedom in how he used his time, working with a community, being able to exercise, and *never again* wearing a suit and tie to work. This list did not, however, point him in any specific direction.

One day he noticed that the battalion chief for the Montgomery County Fire and Rescue Service had parked in front of his house. So he walked outside to find out what was going on. The chief was just checking fire hydrants, but in the course of the conversation, Jerry found out what he'd be doing for the next decade of his life. The chief asked Jerry if he'd thought about becoming a volunteer EMT. He decided to give it a try, though he admits he had no idea what he was getting into. It was harder than he'd imagined. "I really wasn't prepared for the rigor that they put you through to do this job," he said.

Of course, he knew it would be physically challenging, but at fifty-five Jerry was pretty fit (his email name is Speedwalker). It was the mental challenge that was difficult. There was so much to learn. He confessed, "I quit a couple of times. I was bounced out once. It's the first time I've ever been bounced out of anything, and I felt so humiliated. I asked for another chance."

He thought back to the last time he'd really had to open a book and learn stuff—college—so he wrote to his alma mater to order University of Minnesota binders and folders. They helped him get back in the zone. He studied. He learned.

Then came the practical matter of actually doing it. "No one had really showed me how to pull the stretcher out of the back of the ambulance, and it's a little bit complicated," he said. "You have to release the wheels just right or the stretcher will be in free fall. So we pulled the stretcher out, and there was an eighty-year-old woman named Rose on the stretcher, and I didn't release the wheels and Rose fell. I was shocked. I was looking around, thinking, 'Oh my gosh, what have I done to poor Rose?'"

Rose looked up at him and said, "That was exhilarating."

He never made that mistake again, but the guys never let him forget it. "They might make fun of you, but when they make fun of you they're actually accepting you," he said. "If you're not being made fun of, then you're an outsider, and you don't ever want to be an outsider in the firehouse." Finding community was such a driving theme for Jerry that just talking about being accepted as one of the guys in the firehouse brought tears to his eyes.

"The firehouse people are a community," he said. "They live together. They eat together, and they have joy in their life that's very different than any kind of joy I ever felt while I was practicing accounting. They see it all. Life is fleeting to them, and the joy and the way they play outside the firehouse is amazing. It's that community that was really important to me."

How did he win their trust? Simple. After he'd been there a couple of weeks, someone said, "Jerry, it's your turn to clean the toilets," and he did. He was just one of the guys. Most of the guys are professionals. Jerry is an unpaid volunteer, but you wouldn't notice the distinction.

He works two fifteen-hour shifts a week at the Silver Spring, Maryland, firehouse. Seeing him behind the wheel of a four-ton ambulance, you'd never guess that he spent thirty-five years sitting behind a desk. Most volunteers don't drive the ambulance, by the way. Getting certified to drive it required another eighteen months of training.

We've had ample opportunity in recent times to celebrate our heroic first responders—and the journalists among them. I remember the young *Dateline* staffers—some of them interns—who were handed cameras and sent to record the scene on 9/11. Those kids were among the brave journalists who went down to Ground Zero to get the story, and came back changed.

But I'm also thinking of the everyday heroes who routinely answer 911 calls. Like that summer night when the neighborhood kids were playing tag by the light of a moon so full it cast shadows. But squeals of play were suddenly broken by shouting: "Mrs. Trudeau! Mrs. Trudeau!" Tommy was hurt. As shapes and shouts emerged from the shadows, there was Tommy in his big brother's arms (though Ross was still a boy himself). My instincts weren't to run to Tommy but to run to the phone. I called 911 while Ross laid Tommy on the sofa and kept vigil beside him. Help was on the way. While Tommy heaved slow, horrific-sounding breaths, the neighborhood kids explained he'd been running and tripped on cement steps and his windpipe seemed to have taken the blow.

In a flash of blue lights, the sofa was suddenly surrounded by young men and women in uniforms—strong and competent. Tommy was strapped on a paddle wearing a mask attached to an oxygen tank, and we sped to the hospital. By dawn, he was good to go, with a bad bruise and a story to tell.

Jerry has heard stories like mine before. He says sometimes the patient will ask for "the gray-haired guy," assuming he's the most experienced. He's sixty-five now. But his secret is that the work is keeping him young. He has to study, he has to stay fit, but the work feeds his soul. Every day he tries to learn something new.

Still, the thought comes up: how long can he keep at it? Jerry figures that if he can stay on top of the game until he's seventy, he'll be "a happy camper." And then? "The third act."

He's already planning to pull out the whiteboard again and start the process of figuring out his third act.

When I left *Today*, in 1989, we happened to be renovating at home. As we stood together surveying the exposed beams and broken plasterboard littering the floor of what used to be our kitchen, Garry made a dark little joke: "It's sort of a metaphor for your career."

"Yeah," I said. But *I* was smiling.

It's funny. I'm the "change agent," but Gary's the optimist in the family. I'm the one who worries about the what-ifs, and yet, when it's time, I'm eager to go, even when I don't know where, exactly, I'm going.

As I told those young women at Radcliffe (who are well into their forties now): "It feels like a leap of faith to me. For many years I felt like the *Today* show and Jane Pauley were mutually inclusive. Before the twins, the question I was most often asked was 'What time do you get up?' But the question I most feared was 'What will you do *next?*' I'm asked that question now all the time. The truthful answer, I don't know for sure. But I'm smiling."

Changes, that one-hour special I proposed, got record ratings following my highly publicized departure from *Today* and evolved into a series of summer programs, which evolved into a regular weekly newsmagazine called *Real Life with Jane Pauley*.

It was a good idea made better by Executive Producer David Browning (whose name I regularly see on *60 Minutes*)—an exploration of a culture in transition. Though *Real Life* failed as a prime-time newsmagazine, it evolved into *Dateline*. With Stone Phillips and Neal Shapiro, another visionary executive producer, at the helm, this time NBC got it right.

Chapter Six

Daughter of a Musician

We don't always see ourselves as others see us. As a practical matter, we can't. And maybe we don't have such a complete picture of the people who know us best.

Some years ago Hillary Clinton as First Lady was presiding over an event at which one by one, and without notes, she introduced the people onstage. When she came to me, she began, "She's the daughter of a musician . . ." It was awkward. I thought she'd made a mistake; I'm the daughter of a housewife. Suddenly, it hit me—hard enough that later a friend in the audience asked, "What happened up there?" I struggled not to cry as I recognized for the first time in my life: "You *are* the daughter of a musician." Every Sunday of my childhood I'd seen my mother in front of the church facing the congregation—at the organ. I'd played at her feet during choir practice, so I knew about the row of jumbo keys on the floor, and that she played them in her stocking feet. But it had never occurred to me that my mother was a *musician*. That night I called my sister. And Ann (who is supposed to be the *smart one*) said, "Who was Hillary talking about?" Reflecting on this story, I wonder if my mother saw *herself* as a musician. Growing up on a farm in central Indiana, she was said to have practiced piano five hours a day. Five hours a day on a farm where there was always work to do suggests not only that my mother was pretty serious but also that my grandmother was very supportive of her musical ability. Both of my grandparents were members of the church choir, and it must have been a source of pride for them to sing to their daughter's accompaniment.

Evidently, she was encouraged to reach higher. I was surprised when I learned my mother had studied organ at a respected conservatory in Indianapolis. I don't recall she ever spoke about it. She rarely played for the sheer pleasure of it, with the exception of a particular song written in 1915, the year she was born. Watching her fingers dance across the keys in a syncopated confection called "Nola" is my only childhood memory of my mother playing the piano just for fun. And it was never explained (nor had I asked) how all the great sheet music of the 1930s and 1940s—including my favorites, "Stardust" and "Deep Purple"—came to be in our piano bench. What a revelation it was that she had played at a supper club before she was married!

In her senior class "will," beside the names of classmates were words describing how they'd be remembered. The word by my mother's name was "quiet." Providing background music would have suited her perfectly. This also explained the fancy dress outfit she wore on special occasions during my childhood—a lacy black full skirt and matching blouse with rhinestone buttons, which of course she made herself. My mother was undeniably proficient at the piano and organ, but did she think of herself as a musician?

I'll never know for sure, but the weight of evidence points to an answer: not really. In that class will, she described her personal aspirations as "missionary" or "wife." Perhaps being a church musician was connected to service. Maybe practicing piano five hours a day was an expression of her strong affinity for mastering difficult things, like her sewing machine and those complicated patterns she favored.

She was also proficient at an amazing machine called a comptometer. My parents met in an office where she was in charge of accounts payable, running the numbers on this deviously complicated adding machine invented in 1887. I found a twenty-two-page instruction manual for it online. It looks like a typewriter, but it's all numbers—from nine to twenty-seven rows of keys. In the hands of a trained professional, it could be faster than an electronic calculator. I think my mother had a passion for proficiency itself—and proficiency of a particular nature. She seemed to derive deep pleasure from the mastery of mechanical things that required both mental and digital dexterity, and hours and hours of practice.

My mother's story touches on some of the key themes in this book. It underscores a couple of important if counterintuitive insights—for one, that a proficiency is not the same as a passion; and for another, that a close family may be like a tight little forest that obscures the trees—we don't necessarily see each other as others see us. My mother was a timid woman, but her favorite color was red. I don't own red shoes, but I wore her red pumps when I played dress-up. She chose red linoleum tiles for the bathrooms, and the kitchen wallpaper, and the basement floor. On her side of the garage there was a (used) Ford Falcon—red. When she put on her fancy outfit, she painted her nails bright red. Red was her favorite shade of lipstick. Her affinity for the color red suggests a more powerful emotional life than you'd expect in a mild-mannered organist. Shy, timid, quiet—that's what the world saw in Mary Pauley and how she likely saw herself. It's hard to imagine her having a *passion*. But how do you discover a passion that lies unrecognized in the deep purple of still waters?

I began to look at my mother in a different way after Hillary Clinton cast her in a new light. And I've seen over and over—in others and in myself—how a journey of reinvention often helps people connect with a deeper truth about themselves.

Chapter Seven

The Gift

I've always admired my sister, and have been proud to boast of her accomplishments (all the better if they happened to cast a flattering glow upon her nearest relative—me). Ann is really smart. She was Phi Beta Kappa in college—a math major who went on to have a long career at a big brand-name company, where her talent was recognized early. She then became one of the first women to head a high-tech global engineering and manufacturing business. Her accomplishments were substantive, and her unique leadership style was noticed. On one occasion, a top-tier executive of the company, speaking before a large conference of her peers, said, "Ann is like an irreplaceable crystal in a priceless chandelier."

Such an extravagant compliment wrapped in elegant prose is not often heard in corporate settings. I was so proud when she told me, though I had to ask, "What did it mean?"

Ann understood his meaning perfectly. She explained it this way: "It affirmed a skill I knew I had but didn't think was that valuable or even noticed. My position on the leadership team wasn't to shine my own light, but to help others shine." Being paid this public compliment no doubt made her rosy cheeks even rosier at the time, but its effects were long lasting and powerful. She said it had not only validated her strength as a business leader but inspired her to deploy it with greater confidence—and not only at work but also in her community and in her church.

And then she shone her light on me. Ann told me I had a gift for "helping people see themselves in positive and powerful new ways." This was a powerful new way of looking at myself, but just as she had understood the meaning of the chandelier, though I'd never had that thought before, I knew what she meant. As if she'd flipped a switch, her compliment illuminated a thread I could see running throughout my career as a journalist, describing the kinds of stories I thought I did best. "Helping people see themselves in positive and powerful new ways" could have been a mission statement for my daytime show. And what is the purpose of *Your Life Calling* but to help people see the future in some positive and powerful new way? I think everyone has "gifts" like this, but when they are named they become more powerful.

At dinner one evening with my friend Belinda and her husband, Jeffrey, we listened as Jeffrey described a writing exercise that he's made a morning ritual. While some people like to reflect at the end of the day, he writes three pages of top-of-the-mind thoughts from that clear morning channel that gets crowded out in the busyness to come.

I knew about that channel. Listening as Jeffrey and I talked about it, Belinda bemoaned her complete and utter incapacity for introspection. Belinda's engine doesn't idle—that's a fact. She's constantly in the flow. She's already seen everything on, off-, and way-off Broadway. And knows what's coming. She knows what's new and who's news. I'm in awe of her. She's so connected to the world. But that evening she insisted it was all just "noise."

"No!" I said. It's not noise that keeps Belinda's engine racing. It's the *jazz* of life!

Finding clues and making connections that people have yet to recognize for themselves is my favorite part of storytelling.

In a famous commencement address, Steve Jobs talked about connecting the dots. I've always wondered if the undergraduates related to his message as much as their parents did, because as Jobs said, "You can't connect the dots looking forward. You can only connect them looking backwards. So you have to trust that the dots will somehow connect in your future. You have to trust in something—your gut, destiny, life, karma, whatever. This approach has never let me down, and it has made all the difference in my life."

I like to help people connect the dots. For example, Jan Erickson. One of the first things she told me when we met in Boulder, Colorado, was that she never really had a career. She did "a lot of different things. I was in the restaurant management business. I did some children's literacy center work. I did a lot of work with hospice. I was a caregiver. Some jobs were paid, some were volunteer." This piqued my interest, of course, and I started looking for the patterns. As we talked, I began to think the common denominator was the word "service."

Testing my observation, I said, "I'll bet when you were a teenager, you were . . . ," and simultaneously we both said, "a candy striper." Yes, she had been a candy striper. And by the end of the interview, she would see more clearly than I had what her particular gift was.

When she was fifty-two, Jan had a part-time paid position at her church as a care minister for the elderly. In a literal sense, she followed in her father's footsteps. He had been a lay minister at church, too, with a particular interest in visiting the elderly. Both of Jan's parents lost their own parents young—which likely accounts for her father's interest in older people; it definitely accounts for Jan's. As a little girl who didn't have grandparents like the other kids did, she took more notice of older people than most children might have. "I used to go with my dad when he would visit people and I would just observe what this person's life was like, knowing that they had had a really active life at some point, but now their life was pretty small," she said. "Maybe they had their favorite lamp and their favorite chair from their home. And that was kind of it. But what else did they have? And what gave them meaning and dignity?"

As a care minister Jan had become particularly attached to a woman named Jean. "She was incredibly bright. She had graduated from Colorado College in the 1930s, and I would visit her very often," Jan said. Jean had suffered a stroke. It was difficult for her to move her arms. And it offended Jan that this dignified, intelligent woman was relegated to wearing the thing that was easiest to get on her—a hospital gown. "Not only did it lack dignity, but she was cold. And she was quite thin and frail at that point."

Jan was awakened one night by a dream. She had started keeping a dream journal by her bed, so she made a note of her dream and went back to sleep. The next morning, she saw that she'd made a sketch of a jacket. She thought, "What's this about? I can't even sew."

At first she sort of pushed it away, but that dream was relentless. "I would go out for a run and I'd be tweaking the design. I would be sitting at home at night and be thinking about that jacket. I'd wake up thinking about that jacket."

Jan's dream jacket had generous raglan sleeves, to keep the neck and shoulders warm, and a slit up the back, with no buttons. It was a jacket for Jean.

"I think it was a couple of months before I finally said to my husband, 'Jon, I need to talk to you about something, because it's not going away. I need to do something about this.' It was that strong."

Finally, she went to a cut-and-sew manufacturer who made a prototype of her sketch out of recycled Polartec fleece. "It's very lightweight. It's supersoft. It wicks away moisture. It keeps a body comfortable. Whether you're a little too warm or a little too cold, it keeps your body at a good temperature," Jan explained. She took the jacket to Jean. "It slipped on so easily, and she just went, 'Oh, this feels so good.'"

That opened up the floodgates. "All these other ideas tumbled in. I wanted to have a lap blanket that was contoured for the lap, because I saw people with just blankets thrown over them and they would drag on the floor. I wanted something to keep her feet warm. I wanted some leg warmers to keep her legs warm, a jacket with big dolman sleeves to wear if she went out."

Jan had no background in fashion or business, and needless to say neither did her husband. He was a recently retired lawyer. She thinks that worked to their advantage. "One of the things that helped us is we didn't know what we didn't know. And so in some ways it gave us fresh eyes into an industry, and we just asked a lot of questions. It took us a couple of years to do research and development. We'd give samples to caregivers and get feedback from them. And it was all good."

They also wanted to know who else was doing what they were. "You assumed that if it's such a good idea somebody was doing it. And we couldn't find anybody who had done it. And so we just decided we would keep going."

And the "universe" Jan believes in cooperated by sending people to help. "Somebody dropped a business card on my desk and said, 'Check this guy out if you decide you want to build a website.' That guy is still doing our websites today. Somebody else said, 'I know a fashion designer who works at the costume shop at Colorado College. She might be really interested in helping you out.' She has been helping us for ten years."

They finally launched a wellness line of clothing at a Denver trade show. And when fashion buyers were interested too, they realized they were onto something even bigger—universal design. "If you designed for somebody who was less abled, then anybody could wear it," Jan said. "And everyone was drawn to the color, the softness, the comfort."

Today, Janska designs are sold in over 750 boutiques in the United States and Canada. There are two lines—the original wellness line and a much larger fashion line. When they broke a million dollars—after *seven* years—they finally started giving themselves a paycheck, but just one. The real payback came in cards and letters from people saying how much the clothing meant to them, how the wrap was a comfort to their mom in the last stages of her life. "Those kinds of letters just made me know that we are supposed to keep going," Jan said. "They say, 'this matters.'"

Jan believes all of us have ideas, and it's a question of whether or not we ever act on them. "I truly believe that we just lean into this world that we're given and it unfolds exactly as it should. As long as we're paying attention and want it to."

I asked Jan if it could have happened earlier in her life, when she was thirty-two or forty-two. She said, "I don't think so, no. I think that for a long time in my early life I didn't really know that I mattered—that there was something important for me to bring forth in the world. But then later on, as I got older, I realized that my life did matter, and I realized everybody has a gift; everybody comes to this planet with something to give."

How incongruous that in her sixties a care minister found her calling in fashion. At the end of our conversation, Jan and I returned to my idea that service was the underlying theme of her life, but she recognized now that it was service of a particular kind. Jan decided that her gift was "finding ways to make people comfortable."

I think everyone has gifts waiting to be discovered. But I've come to understand this process of self-discovery in a new way. When I wrote my memoir some years ago, I saw it as a journey of self-discovery. Implicit in the project and explicit in my message was that self-discovery would be the prerequisite to a successful reinvention. But now I see it the other way around. For me, and for many of the people I've profiled, self-discovery is not the prerequisite to reinvention. It's the payoff.

• • •

I had already launched *Your Life Calling* when my sister shared her insight about my gift for helping people see themselves in positive and powerful new ways. But it was validation that I was on the right path. The objective of *Your Life Calling*, the TV series and this book, is to inspire people through storytelling to imagine their own future in powerful and positive ways.

Self-discovery is the reward for taking a step toward reinvention. And even a false step may give you a fresh perspective on yourself. But having that perspective articulated in a phrase—"help others shine" . . . "make people comfortable" . . . "see themselves in a positive new way" . . . "the jazz of life"—is affirming, validating, and confidence building.

Sue Halpern is a college professor and writer. Her one-paragraph bio concludes with the sentence, "I'm the human half of a therapy-dog team, was a Rhodes Scholar and a Guggenheim Fellow, and remain hopeful that ice cream is the key to world peace." I think you'd like her as much as I did. She has a self-deprecating charm and down-to-earth way of saying wise things. "I think that people are often unaware of their capacities," she said. "And in part because everyone is tired and everyone gets into whatever routine that they get into, it's only when they get shaken out of it that they start asking questions of themselves—like, 'What am I capable of?' Or, 'What do I really want?' Or, 'Where should I be?'"

Her latest book, *A Dog Walks into a Nursing Home*, was inspired by a common event that shook her out of her routine.

Her daughter went away to college, and her husband travels a lot in his work. "Suddenly," she said, "there was a silence I had never heard before. The quiet almost became a noise—it was like another presence in my life. I was like, what am I supposed to be doing now?" Sue experienced this "emptiness" in a surprising way. She described it as "a gift box that I could fill somehow." She ticked off some options: stay home and watch golf, go shopping, learn a language, become a gardener. But Sue explained she was aiming for something that would take her a little further outside herself—to try something she'd never done before.

Sue shared this very quiet house with a seven-year-old Labradoodle named Pransky. "I think she was bored. It was like she needed a job." Sue researched how the two of them could become a certified therapy team. "Going to the nursing home, that was the new thing in my life, being in that setting, having to interact with strangers, having to interact with strangers who are ill."

"Would you describe that as out of your comfort zone?" I asked Sue.

She replied, "I would describe that as *a lot* out of my comfort zone."

A nursing home seemed like a perfect fit for Pransky. She knew her dog would thrive on connecting with people, but to become a certified therapy dog Pransky would have to master fifteen new behaviors. "The dog needs to be able to walk by food and not go for it. The dog needs to be able to be left alone—in this test I think it was three minutes with you out of sight and not make any noise. No pulling on a leash, no straining, no whining, no barking. Complete silence." And this was a test with one passing grade: perfect. "I actually was pretty convinced that we were going to fail," Sue admitted, "but I was very committed to trying."

Pransky was a country girl. She'd spent her whole life exploring the woods and she'd never even been on a leash. After months of training, as the day of the test neared it didn't look promising. On test day, she took Pransky on a ten-mile run so she was one tired puppy, but Sue says Pransky was the best-trained dog there. She aced the test.

They reported for work at a local nursing home. Sue was pretty nervous, but Pransky was a natural. For four years they've been a familiar presence. "People just lighten up, brighten up. They are getting this feeling of connectedness, this feeling of joy, which is unexpected. My dog becomes a kind of jumping-off point to remember things that are really happy."

They work one day a week for two hours, which doesn't sound like much, but it's *hard* work—for Pransky. "The people at the nursing home told me that it was going to be exhausting for the dog," Sue said. "And I thought, 'You don't know my dog. My dog doesn't get exhausted.'" But being a therapy dog is mentally exhausting. Pransky is constantly paying attention to Sue for cues, while people are touching her tail or pulling on her ears. "She lets them do whatever it is they're going to do, and she knows that's what she's supposed to be doing." After the first day

Pransky slept all the way home. And at home she slept the rest of the day.

Two hours a week isn't a big time commitment for Sue, but volunteering pays very real dividends. As a writer and journalist she's uncovered interesting research. "This is going to sound really crazy, but people who volunteer actually end up feeling richer—as if they had more money in their pocket," she said. And studies show that life expectancy gets longer if you volunteer. "It doesn't require you to have money. It doesn't require you to do anything very radical. But I think what happens is that people realize that they have things that they can share that are just intrinsic to who they are."

Just like dogs do.

That you might have to be "reintroduced" to yourself is not an original idea, though a dozen years ago it was new to me. My sister facilitated the introduction with the woman I grew up to be.

I always enjoyed the business books Ann packed in her suitcase when we traveled together. In my memoir, I described one in particular, *Now, Discover Your Strengths*, by Marcus Buckingham and Donald O. Clifton. The premise was that most people have a closer acquaintance with their weaknesses than with their strengths. The things we're best at "just come naturally," and we might take them for granted. My weaknesses, however, were like speed bumps I stumbled over every day. I knew them intimately, but struggled to name a single strength. This book was a bestseller for years, so there must be a lot of us who feel the same way.

The book came with a special code for an online "Strengths-Finder" test. At Ann's urging I took it, presuming it would confirm my conviction that I had *none*. I'm serious. Thirty minutes later I was holding a printout of some pretty strengthy-sounding words: Strategic. Command. Ideation. Activator. I said, "This isn't me. It's G.I. Jane!" (I noticed Ann and Garry exchange a knowing glance, suggesting they were acquainted with this G.I. Jane.) I wasn't wrong, I was just half right; both images are correct. But the person I saw in the mirror was probably not the person you may have seen on TV.

On the first day of second grade, my teacher, Mrs. Cooper, referred to her class list and called me Margaret. My full name is Margaret Jane Pauley, but I'd never been called anything but Janie in my life. I didn't correct her, and I went through the entire year known as Margaret.

For decades I persisted in clinging to the idea that I was shy. I was even diagnosed by a doctor: Dr. Phil. During an interview for a *Dateline* profile, Phil McGraw claimed *he* was shy. Seeing my incredulity, he added, "And so are you! I've seen that in you for years, girl." The incongruity of two "shy" people having a comfortable chat with three TV cameras pointed at them should say something about the duality—to say the least—of personality.

Afterward, Phil and I went to Central Park to shoot the standard TV walkabout material known as "B roll." When the cameraman said he had all he needed, I walked with Dr. Phil to the street to wait for his car and driver. After three hours of non-stop talk *on* camera, we stood together for several minutes—two shy people, in total silence.

It's my understanding that, in most personality traits, people sit somewhere on a spectrum. For example, I took a test in a *Time* magazine article about shyness that suggested I was neither introvert nor extrovert, but, like the majority of people, I was an "ambivert"—meaning a little of both. And these days I see more of this G.I. Jane. She gets out more. She gets things done. She's writing this book.

On the eve of Prince William's marriage to Kate Middleton, Tom Brokaw and I were reminiscing on *Today* about covering the wedding of Prince Charles and Diana. I remembered there'd been some concern that the bride, her dress with its twenty-five-foot train, and her very large father might not squeeze into that Cinderella coach. That's when it first occurred to me—thirty years after the wedding—that a nineteen-year-old girl known worldwide as Shy Di had personally ordered up the most famous look-at-me dress of the twentieth century! Yet we persisted in calling her *shy*. And she no doubt persisted in thinking she was.

Labels can get attached to us and we accept them and live with them whether they're true or not—or only part of the story.

Like my sons' childhood superhero action figure toys, everyone comes with a different profile of strengths. Nobody has them all. Scanning the StrengthsFinder list for other "strengths," I took particular note of one called "woo"—defined as winning people over and making them respond to you and love you. Woo was definitely not on my list, but I'll bet it would be on Barbara Walters's. And Diane Sawyer's, too. Woo is what it takes to lure a *get*—the big newsmaker interview that wins the ratings race. I was woefully weak at woo, but I wish I had spent less time in my life worrying about how much more successful I might have been if I had been a little more like Barbara Walters. Or Diane Sawyer. Or Katie Couric. I was pretty successful at being Jane Pauley. But I was always being compared to the best of the best—at something or other that they happened to do best. Of course, it was mostly *me* doing the comparing.

Chapter Eight

The Next Act

B rigadier General, Retired, Anthony Tata still exudes command presence, but he wears his authority in such an unassuming manner I got over the inclination to salute pretty quickly. It took a while longer to get used to calling him Tony. He'd been in the military since 1967, when he was seventeen—a high school athlete seeking physical challenge, and that was West Point. Though he looked comfortable wearing a suit and tie, it surely had been an adjustment; he'd been out of uniform barely a year. "In the military we talk about the difference between an occupation or profession and a calling," he told me. "An occupation is about paying the bills. A profession is about having a body of standards. A calling is about serving an idea that transcends yourself. The military was my calling."

After the Point, he chose another challenge—infantry. In a

warrior culture, combat experience accelerates promotions, and Tony rose through the ranks quickly. A young brigadier general, he had begun contemplating life after thirty-two years in the U.S. Army. He was looking for a new challenge.

"One lifetime for me is too short to do all the things that you can do and make all the contributions that you can make," he said. Why settle for one career, when he figured there was time enough to have two? Tony was young enough at forty-nine—and certainly fit enough—to try to fit two lifetimes into one.

The question was, what next? It may surprise you to know that the U.S. Army helps officers answer questions like that.

The General Officer Transition Course is designed to help career military transition to civilian life. In Tony's words, "It was for people who it had been thirty years or so since they bought a suit or submitted a résumé." He described a group of retiring military officers arranged in a horseshoe around a discussion leader who posed questions like, "What motivates you?" When the leader asked, "If you could do anything you wanted, what would it be?" Tony says the room went silent. "I think a lot of it was that people were just totally, one hundred percent immersed in and dedicated to what they were doing, and maybe they were doing the thing that they most wanted to do. And so they hadn't given any thought to the second act." He said that the most common answer was "I'm not sure."

Tony had led similar conversations with men and women under his command many times, and he knew the drill. "When people are looking for a calling and a purpose in life, you start with who you really are and where you are in your life—like a land navigation course. There's no way you can get to the point you're going, if you don't know where you are. What I do and what I've done with my troops before is sit across from them and work through that and do it in a methodical way to where it's not just a joke or a game, or another drill that you're doing. You bare your soul a little bit. It's important."

When it was his turn to answer the question "What is it that you want your second act to be?" he said, "I want to be a novelist." There was some snickering around the room, until he mentioned his multibook deal with a publisher. During his downtime downrange, he'd published three novels. Writing, he said, "was a way for me to just open up a typewriter or a notebook and escape into another world, because it's a pretty tough world you live in, in the military." He donates his book royalties to the USO Hospital Services Fund.

But something else was calling him. He described to me a life-changing incident in Afghanistan in 2006. "We were getting ready to do an air assault operation up into the Hindu Kush mountains, and a rocket landed in a schoolyard in Asadabad killing one teacher and several children. And it was an Al-Qaeda rocket that landed in the middle of the schoolyard. The commanding general turned to me and said, 'Tony, you're a writer, let's get an article out real quick on this.' Thirty minutes later, I had a research team that found the Taliban had gone after about one hundred and twenty schools and had killed fifty teachers. These guys didn't want the Afghan children to learn; they didn't want them to have access to education. I had this crystallized moment where I thought, 'The enemy of my enemy is education.'"

By happenstance, just as he was preparing to retire, Tony heard from the Broad Foundation. The foundation handpicks people from nonacademic professions to be trained to become superintendents of urban school districts. Tony was urged to apply, though he was told that from two hundred prospects, only sixteen would be chosen. Tony Tata likes a challenge, so of course he applied, and he was accepted. He thought it was the right fit: "I like being in charge, I like running large organizations, I love building good teams, and I love a good mission and good people." I've read that the majority of teachers have had a parent who taught school. Both of Tony's parents are educators.

While this leader of men was in training to become a leader of children, he took on the role of CFO of Washington, D.C.'s troubled school system. He said, "As a general, I could snap my fingers and three thousand, five thousand, ten thousand troops would change their uniform or whatever. And here, you've got to build consensus and you've got to clearly articulate what the mission is and what you expect them to do. And it doesn't matter what you've done before, it's what you're doing for them today."

When his training was complete, Tony sought his first position as a school superintendent and was headed for Raleigh, North Carolina.

In general, retiring military officers have more than the usual options. Corporations covet their experience as managers, logistics experts, and leaders. Tony might have had some lucrative opportunities. Knowing he had two college-age kids, I asked, "Why didn't you make the money decision more paramount?" He had a simple answer. "At the end of the day, Jane, it's not what we take, it's what we give."

Chapter Nine

Finding Balance

You might remember a social psychologist named Richard Luker from an earlier chapter. He collects data about how Americans spend our leisure time. He's one of the foremost experts in the field. Ironically, he spent very little of his time in leisure. He liked his work, but there wasn't "play" in his life. And yet he told me, "It was somewhere around fifty when I recognized I had this capacity to live significantly longer, and with greater vitality than my parents did." And then several years later, he had what he calls his "softball moment." Outdoors on a gorgeous Florida day, as he tells the story, there was a cell phone to his ear and his mind was on work when something caught his eye. He noticed guys about the same age as he was playing softball. Richard loves sports, but for decades he'd been on the spectator side of the action. He told the story with tears in his eyes, how he peered through the chain-link fence like the eleven-year-old he'd been forty-something years before. He wanted to play! Richard can't remember if he said good-bye to the person on the phone or even hung up, but something profound was calling to him, and he decided to listen.

He recognized that day how out of balance he was. It was a ridiculous irony, because Richard is a professor of recreation psychology, who had no recreation in his life.

Richard didn't quit his job, but he changed his life. He added play to it. He joined a softball league and got back in balance. Now twice a week he puts on a uniform and plays ball with the guys. He was pretty nervous in the beginning, but after he hit a double, the second baseman, a retired firefighter from Pittsburgh, gave him a pat on the back and said, "Nice hit, kid."

Richard speaks from both personal and professional experience when he says work and play to the exclusion of all else are both "four-letter" words. A healthy life needs balance.

Early morning, Monterey Bay, California. I step out onto my hotel room balcony and look down at the beach. A man is at work with a shovel. In swift, strong movements, he flings one shovelful of sand after another on top of a large mound. It looks like backbreaking work. After six or seven shovelfuls, he stops, takes a brief break, then starts again. It is beautiful to watch. It's also why I am here—to get to know this sand man and his work.

Reinvention can take many forms. Kirk Rademaker is a sand carver—a line of work you've probably never heard of because it didn't exist until about five years ago. How he came to be a professional sand carver—one of the best in the world, in fact—seems unusual. But as he put it when we met that day, his reinvention was a "convergence" of many things in his life experience. While it's unlikely you'll be inspired to become a sand carver, too, Kirk may inspire you to think about that idea of convergence—when everything you've done before meets up in some entirely new way. And you are renewed. That's Kirk's story.

As Kirk approached fifty, it was a dark time for him. He was going through a divorce, and though he had a good job as project manager of a cabinet shop in Oakland, California, it was very stressful. "When the phone rings it's not somebody saying, 'You did a great job, everything fit, it was perfect,'" he said. "It's an angry person demanding to know where the cabinets are or telling you they don't fit or that something else went wrong." Life was taking a toll. He retreated into art. He'd always found solace in drawing and made elaborate and fanciful pencil sketches late into the night. But he was becoming isolated and socially withdrawn, and for the first time Kirk felt depressed. As he put it, "My head—everything was just dark in there."

One day he took a solitary walk on a beach. On a whim, he started to build a sand castle. He'd read a book called *The Art of Sandcastling* by Ted Siebert, and he'd had a fleeting thought that it might be fun to do. But it was so much more. "It was like the sun rising on all the horizons at once," he said. "I can't describe that feeling. I knew that beach was going to change my life."

As he worked, people stopped to watch and marvel: "Oh, that's cool, man, that's really cool." He said, "I was being creative. I was talking to people."

Sand became Kirk's weekend de-stressor. He discovered there was a little community of sand carvers, and he couldn't wait to get to the beach. He was surprised by how much he enjoyed the social aspect. "The sand basically took me by the scruff of the neck and threw me out into the world with people."

I ask him if anyone ever told him he was crazy. "Oh, yes. I would go back to the office on Monday and our office manager would say, 'Kirk, you live in a fantasy world out there.' But I'd disagree. The beach was reality, how life should be. The office, in our cubicles staring at computer screens, was synthetic."

It went on this way for about a year, until one day as Kirk worked in his office in West Oakland with a view of a treeless, oil-stained industrial street, his phone rang. This time it wasn't an unhappy client but a girlfriend from the beach community of sand carvers. Good news! She and Kirk had been invited to a sand carving event—in Italy!

Kirk slumped in his chair. It was impossible. He'd never been to Europe, and he'd always wanted to go, but he had five projects lined up in the shop, and no time off coming. It was a terrible disappointment, but he had to say no. He felt hand-cuffed, but in his disappointment, he was determined to find a way to be free. He gave himself six months to wind down his obligations, quit his job, and transition full-time to sand sculpting. And he did it.

He moved to an area of Santa Cruz that really, truly is called Happy Valley. And now he makes a living as a sand carver. In the first year Kirk earned about two thirds of his cabinetmaking salary. But in the second year he earned two thirds more. He gets hired for marketing events, for team-building exercises at conventions, and to create cultural symbols for cities and countries and corporations. His client roster includes Google, Yahoo, Apple, Toyota, the American Cancer Society, the Girl Scouts, and Lucasfilm. But the real payoff was finding himself.

Kirk's story may look like an extreme makeover, but he doesn't see it that way. He calls it a *convergence* of everything he had ever done and ever learned. "I had been to art school, I was a carpenter, I had made things all my life," he explained. "And when I started doing the sand, I was making something, I was using my creative skills, and it seemed so natural."

His drafting table is a beach. The tools of his trade are shovels and carving knives instead of tracing paper, a ruler, and a T square. But he's still designing and building things. And he's putting his old fine arts degree to use in a way he'd never imagined. Those intricate pencil sketches he still does late at night are often the inspirations for three-dimensional carvings in sand. His signature style is both whimsical and elaborate. He says his inspiration is Dr. Seuss.

"I don't really feel qualified to give advice or to give people a message," he said, "but for me it's almost like I took everything I ever learned and tried to have the innocence of a child, tried to be a kid again, to have that same outlook on life and the future." He recalled his childhood in the Central Valley of California. "I used to build little forts out of the dirt clods and twigs. So I'm doing the same thing." It was a convergence.

More than a new career, he thinks he's found a new outlook on life. "I spent my life trying to make something permanent— my relationships, my house," he explained. "I put so much energy into that permanence. And as soon as I abandoned that, as soon as I went and did something that's totally impermanent, and really put my heart and soul in it, the world opened up to me."

A sand sculpture is built in a day and not intended to last much longer. Sometimes the sand doesn't cooperate at all. Kirk describes some of the spectacular collapses he's suffered. But he calls the impermanence and unpredictability part of the "charm" of the medium. "Just like life," he added. "Sometimes you work hard on something and then it collapses and you just start over again."

That morning before we met, when I watched Kirk piling up shovelfuls of sand on the beach, he was at work on something special for our *Your Life Calling* segment. At the end of our interview he unveiled it—the *Today* logo carved in sand. I recognized that it was not only an example of his talent but a perfect statement of Kirk Rademaker's new perspective on life. It didn't say "tomorrow," it didn't say "next year," it didn't say "forever." It just said "*today*."

Anyone can make a sand castle, although not everyone can make a career out of doing it like Kirk has. But it might just be fun. The takeaway is that we all have skills and experience and knowledge accrued over our lifetimes that might be deployed in some remarkable new way. A convergence as Kirk defined it is a big idea. But he left me with another, smaller one that could transform anyone's life.

He said, "I think what a person should do if they are really dissatisfied is just find something that is therapy to them—music or some art form that resonates with them. It doesn't have to be sand, it could be music, drawing. It could be a conversation, something that feeds your soul, that gets you excited. And don't quit your job, but just try to make that a bigger part of your life because that is going to give you the balance that you need."

There's a postscript to my day on the beach with Kirk Rademaker.

Arriving at the hotel the night before, I put the key in the lock and opened the door, unprepared for the happy face of a big full moon waiting to greet me. It was breathtaking. I walked straight to the window overlooking Monterey Bay, sparkling with moonlight, and opened the balcony door to the sound of crashing of waves on the beach. I shot a little video on my smartphone and sent it to Garry. I've sent the family pictures from hotel rooms before, but this time he replied: "You really *are* seeing the country!"

It's not merely that I travel more. I see more. I notice things. I notice how I've changed.

For most of my career, travel was one of the most obvious perks of my job. I literally saw the world. I do appreciate how lucky I've been. Photos don't lie—I was as happy as I appeared to be in those glamorous locations. But I rarely wanted to *go*. For me, getting there was not half the fun, it was ninety percent of the problem. For one thing, I hated packing (still do). For another, the most interesting people I knew were the husband and three small children I was leaving behind. I felt guilty leaving home, but I also felt guilty and ungrateful for not wanting to go. And the glamour of being "on assignment" has a downside: it is after all, an *assignment*.

These days, I travel more than ever, but I no longer have the tug and pull of small children at home. And while not all of my destinations are as beautiful as Monterey Bay, the number one revelation of my reinvention has been this: when I send myself, I can't wait to go.

Chapter Ten

In Alignment

N ot long ago, I was chatting with my doctor while he exam-
ined my sore thumb. He asked what I was up to these days,
blending the word "arthritis" nonchalantly into the conversation.
(*Arthritis?*)

I told him about *Your Life Calling* and reinvention, and he
said, referring to himself and his doctor colleagues, "That's *all* we
talk about." I got the impression that nothing was lining up in
front of them.

Peter Drucker studied and taught leadership for more than
fifty years. His name is usually accompanied by the words "leg-
endary" or "guru." My sister probably introduced me to his land-
mark book, *The Effective Executive.*

In one of his last interviews with *Forbes* magazine, Drucker,
who was then ninety-five, said, "The worst midlife crisis happens

to physicians, as you know." I guess I can see why. The healing profession is often a calling, and it must be hard to follow your own act when you've had a calling.

Rick Rittmaster felt called when he was ten years old. He thought about God and spiritual things more than most ten-year-olds. He told me he wanted to work with people and "a parish ministry is the primary way I envisioned that." But after college he joined the Air Force because "I didn't feel like I'd proven myself. It was the challenge. But this call to ministry, you know, kept pulling me." And so he went to seminary. As senior pastor at a Lutheran church in Minnesota, he'd been in parish ministry for fifteen years and believed he was doing the work he was called to do, until he began to feel like he was "drying out." I intuited his meaning, though I'd never heard it described that way.

It seems that being senior pastor of a large church is a lot like being CEO of a large organization. Administration, operations, personnel, fundraising all began to eclipse the pastoral work and counseling that had called Richard to the ministry and nourished his own soul. This wasn't the work he'd been called to do.

As a pastor Rick liked to call on parishioners (with their permission) at their places of work—not only because it's harder to find busy people at home these days, but also because he was as interested in knowing what they *did* as in knowing where they lived.

"What if they were in the wrong job?" I asked. "What if

you visited them at work and you could tell, this is eating them alive?"

"Well, I would talk to them about that: 'How is this feeding your soul?' Now here's Pinocchio"—he laughed ruefully—"because I wasn't aware of just how much I was drying out at the same time."

Newly divorced and feeling overwhelmed by the pressures of his life and work, Rick remembered a concerned friend asking him, "What do you like to do for fun?" He was embarrassed to have no answer. It felt like a cloud had descended on him. He couldn't concentrate. He could hardly get out of bed. He went to a doctor, describing how he felt overwhelmed, distracted, and weepy. The doctor recognized the symptoms of depression, prescribed medication, and suggested that he take a couple of weeks off. "It was right around Christmastime," he said. "I'll never forget it."

He went home and lay down on a sofa, watching the snow fall outside. "It was a profound experience for me, because what I got was a sense that this depression was saying to me, 'You're gonna lay down there on that couch and you're gonna think about your life. And when you get it straight in your head about what it is you want to do, then you can get up.' Instead of fighting it, I cooperated with it. I began listening to my life. I know it sounds like a midlife crisis, and you could call it that."

Rick makes a strong connection between what we *do* and how we *feel*. Looking back, he said, "I was a pretty good preacher." He loved teaching and interacting with people, but he wondered, "How many religious leaders go into ministry with the idea that they're going to be really great administrators?"

After four days he got off the couch having made a decision. He resigned the ministry. He called it both the scariest and the most mature thing he'd done in his life. Some might think he was running away, but he saw it as "running *toward*."

He went back to school to get a master's degree in counseling. It was about empowering people. "It was about helping get them unstuck as I was experiencing myself getting unstuck." In the meantime, he needed to make some money. He laughed recalling the day a former parishioner found him tending bar at a country club and imagined her thinking, "So, it's come to *this*."

It was his son's idea to check out Craigslist. And that's where Rick saw an advertisement that piqued his interest. It was a vague job description about giving spiritual support to young people. When he called the number, he found out it was the Minnesota National Guard Chaplain Corps. "To me, it was God saying, 'This is the step now.' I didn't have to think twice about it." Having been in the Air Force, Rick had an affinity for working with soldiers. But before he signed the papers he was reminded, "You know you're going into a war zone." Three military chaplains have died in the line of duty in Iraq and Afghanistan, including one from Minnesota. Undaunted, he signed up.

Two months later, at forty-nine, he was a chaplain in the United States Army. And in 2009 Captain Richard Rittmaster was deployed to Iraq and assigned to a forward operating base. After rocket and mortar attacks, he counseled the wounded and the dying. "I can still see their faces. It's not something you get over."

Part of Rick's job now is ministering to other military chaplains because like the soldiers they serve, chaplains bring the battlefield home. He told me of a dream he'd had just the previous night. It was a military ceremony, and he was asked to give an invocation. "But I started to cry. I couldn't get the words out."

Later, he took me to visit a memorial in honor of the fallen warriors at Fort Hood. He spoke softly but resolutely. "There's great sadness in the world, and being a chaplain, my role, my journey, is not to deny it or to resist it, but to accept it and to mourn with those who mourn."

There will be another chapter in Rick's journey. He thinks he'll most likely be in private counseling, in a clinic, or maybe part-time in a church. Working with people, helping people, is still the work he feels called to do and the work that nourishes his own soul. "What I am committed to doing is exactly what I did before, to listen for what gives me life and generates enthusiasm."

He told me about a book he'd read, *Let Your Life Speak*, by Parker Palmer, who says our sense of vocation does not come through willfulness, it comes through listening. "And I had not been listening to my life," Rick explained.

I added my own observation: "When you're not listening,

the voice you're not listening to finds other ways to get your attention."

He agreed. "And it got my attention in a real significant way. In my last year of ministry, I had a plant that was green and vibrant and growing, and then I put out a vase with some rocks in it and a dead twig, and I thought these are two different ways that our soul can be. If we're feeding our soul, it's going to be green and vibrant and growing. If we're not engaged in the kinds of things that really give us life, if we neglect them, we dry out. I'm not talking about hedonism. I'm talking about living in such a way that we are in alignment."

I heard a distant bell ringing when Captain Rittmaster spoke that word, "alignment." It's key to my thinking about reinvention and has been since I first heard it just over a decade ago. It was a major turning point in my life. I told Rick the story I wrote about in *Skywriting*. The setting was my first parents' weekend at college as a parent, in a lecture hall filled with other fifty- and sixty-somethings. The professor was explaining the concept of "good work"—not to be confused with "good works" (which the late author John Gardner defined as "when excellence and ethics meet").

"Good work" in academic circles describes work that is nourishing, not enervating. Its main component, as the professor wrote in big red letters on a whiteboard, is being in ALIGNMENT with the mission or product of your work. After eleven years on

Dateline, an award-winning newsmagazine, I did not feel it. I think it was the growing emphasis on the "get"—the big newsmaker interview that pulls the big ratings—that threw me out of alignment. It's good work if you can get it—and I imagine highly rewarding if you're the best at it, like Barbara Walters, who, as I've said before, is the champion of woo. I'd felt unhappy and out of sync, and now understood why. In that lecture hall, I decided it was time to go.

Ironically, walking away from *Dateline* may have made me a "get." I got a call from Barbara Walters. You know you've "arrived" when Barbara calls, except that I was "leaving." *TV Guide* called me "the poster child for second acts." Everyone wanted to know why I was leaving. I explained that I thought there was something more for me—more freedom, more independence, more meaning, though I understood that *more* might appear to be *less*. And nobody thought I was crazy. But a funny thing happened on my way out the door. All that publicity over my leaving made NBC reluctant to say good-bye.

So, even as *Dateline* prepared a big farewell testimonial, NBC confidentially approached me with an offer—a daytime show of my own. It was definitely *more*, not less. I had a decision to make.

Chapter Eleven

Packing for a Long Trip

When my friend Meg asked, "What am I going to *do* for forty years?" I remarked that she looked like a woman who suddenly realized she hadn't packed enough for a long trip. That's how I got to thinking about packing for the future.

I've seen it said that when test subjects are asked to imagine themselves in the future, their MRI brain scans light up in the same pattern as when people are asked to think of a stranger. So, on behalf of that stranger who is you in the future, let's think a bit about what you might want to have when the future arrives, because it's likely to be longer than you think.

Packing, as I've said, is one of my least favorite things. But one weekend I began making an inventory of things my future self might be happy to have. I made a list of favorite things, places, and songs; a list of things I did well or could learn to do better. Back when I was forty-five and started playing golf, I looked forward to being able to say at sixty-five, "I've been playing golf for twenty years!" I'm getting close, and though I still don't have a handicap, who's counting? I still wouldn't call myself a golfer, but I'm glad I play golf.

I could certainly become a better cook. Years ago, I was playing with my daughter Rickie, and when I said, "Mommy has to get dinner now," she asked if she could "press the buttons." I don't aspire to be as gifted at cooking as my friends Meg and Katy or Diane and Ellen are, but I might focus on three or four entrées and some desserts that my future grandchildren would look forward to. It might be fun to have my friends teach me.

Jane Austen could be on my list. I've been rereading Jane Austen novels I'd not read since high school, or thought I'd read when I'd only seen a movie. I could make a specialty of Jane Austen. Rickie and I read every book the nineteenth-century author Wilkie Collins wrote. That was fun to do together. Joining a book club is on my list of things my future self will be very grateful I have done. Being part of a social network strongly correlates with well-being. And I take great pleasure in the titles I'm amassing on my e-reader. I don't always remember what I've read, but my future self will be very happy to have cultivated a habit of reading. I hope it makes me a more interesting grandma, just in case I never learn how to cook anything delicious.

This packing concept may also include lists of things to let go of. When Arianna Huffington celebrated her fiftieth birthday, she said she released herself from the goal of learning German, which her mother was fluent in. At one point, I wanted to learn how to play bridge. My friend Joan plays duplicate bridge several times a week, and another friend, Ellen, set a goal and became a life master. But bridge is not on my list. Why take extra baggage into the future?

The Salon.com columnist Cary Tennis has also thought about the packing metaphor. A middle-aged woman posted a question to his advice column. She wanted to know how she could best enjoy the rest of her life, and he wrote, "You can't see all of your life. It has a horizon, but it's not round like the earth . . . you can't get high enough to see the future. So you pack for the unforeseen. . . . You're talking about a planned arrival in a strange land. So you pack carefully."

Tennis listed some things you might want to have for such a trip: a regimen and a routine, a thing you do that always works when things go wrong, a song that gives you goose bumps, a certain walk on a certain path that always elevates your spirits, a meditation that always calms you, a food you always like to eat, somebody you can always call.

For me, that person would be my sister, Ann, who noticed that this list was mostly about things that give "peace of mind."

I was looking for Ann's feedback and emailed my ideas about packing for this trip. Being five days from her sixtieth birthday at the time, she responded the same day. "You've given me a great idea! I know how I'll be spending the weekend. I'm working on a list of things to pack for a birthday box. I look forward to opening the box!"

For the next three days Ann thought about the precious things in her life—things that gave her peace of mind, or inspiration, things that lifted her spirits, touchstones to cherished memories, little objects, precious photographs. It may surprise you to know that she didn't open the box on her birthday. It's been five years, and she's still never opened it. The project of filling her birthday box was enough. The project transformed anxiety over a "big" birthday into a pulse of creative energy and a celebration of the life she'd made and the person she'd become. Filling a birthday box was like building a bridge from one phase of her life into the next. She crossed the bridge with peace of mind.

My sister's response to the idea of packing for a long trip was buoyant. Sometimes the question makes people pensive. It always makes them think.

Thanks to Garry and Ann Kolbell (my closest associate at NBC and closest friend), my future self will have organized binders filled with articles and magazine covers—a testament to a career that deserves more respect than I've been inclined to give it. But I might add to this a photo binder of four decades of changing hairstyles. I was blessed with great hair and cursed with bad hairdos, with nobody to blame but myself. My friends Katy and Belinda took me to see a critically acclaimed documentary film in commercial release about the fashion icon Diana

Vreeland called *The Eye Has to Travel*, because I was in it, having interviewed her in the early eighties. When I first appeared on the screen I literally screamed. What was that getup I was wearing? And my hair! My claim to have coined the phrase "bad hair day" has never been refuted. My future self, and those hoped-for grandchildren, will surely find the evolution of my look endlessly amusing. I must remember to pack that.

Catherine Silverman is an expert on packing. I'm not speaking in metaphors now. She grew up the daughter of a foreign correspondent and lived all over the world. Moving every few years was a way of life for her family, but her mother had a flair for decorating and a gift for making every new house feel like home. Catherine inherited her mother's talent. Her home is lovely and filled with beautiful things. While many of us, like Betsy McCarthy, have discovered the joy of traveling light, Catherine is acquiring more and more. She reinvented herself as a home stager at age fifty-eight. A stager is hired to prep houses for sale by sprucing them up with temporary furniture. She showed me the *eight* lockers she rents to store all her stuff.

The first thing you notice is the birdcage. No wonder it caught her eye at a flea market. It's very beautiful. And very large. "I had absolutely no idea where I was ever going to use that birdcage," she said. "Every time I get a new project, I think, 'I wonder if I'm going to be able to use the birdcage this time.'"

Her storage lockers are filled with lamps in pairs and singles, and sisal rugs in a dozen sizes. She has suites of upholstered chairs and sofas. And beds and bedspreads and headboards. And dining tables and chairs. And end tables and occasional tables. And objects and art—things that make a house look like a home, but not *your* home. (A tip from the pro: If you're downsizing and selling a home, take down the family pictures and store away the personal mementos. People want to picture *their* family in the house not yours.)

Because she's staging several houses at any given time, Catherine has to have a large and varied inventory. I asked her where she did her shopping, and she laughed. "Shopping? Let's use that term kind of loosely, because shopping might mean you're driving by a Dumpster one day and you see two chairs, and you screech to a halt and you put those chairs in your car, which I have done." And so have I!

I take particular pleasure in moving furniture—mine or yours! Years after the fact, my nephew Zach still talks about the time Aunt Jane came to visit and was ready to leave for the airport with my suitcases packed when she decided the sofa was in the wrong place. In twenty minutes I had rearranged my sister's entire living room.

I love moving things around to see how different arrangements work. I once moved a piano from one room to another—by myself. Garry wasn't home, but he would not have been eager to help. It's not that he's indifferent to decor. He's got a better eye than I have. But he likes things to stay put. We had a running difference of opinion over the boys' Lego projects long ago and Garry's penchant for *gluing* the pieces together.

You can only imagine how my heart sang when our son Ross emailed me a video of his new bedroom furniture and *solicited* my advice on how to arrange the room. Nobody else would ask for my decorating advice, much less pay for it. Having an affinity for moving furniture is probably a prerequisite for a stager, but so is talent.

Catherine has talent. But becoming a stager happened for her—as reinvention often does—in stages.

After college she had a pretty glam job as press secretary to a U.S. senator. After she married and started a family, she was a stay-at-home mom, though in her words, "I wasn't staying home every day waiting for the school bus to pull in. You have to keep certain things alive in yourself."

Her flair for design is obvious in her own home, so it was natural that friends would ask for advice, and that segued into a little freelance interior decorating. But it was not a good fit. For one thing, decorating is about the *client's* taste (or lack thereof). For another thing, as Catherine says, "The job never ends." There was always another pillow, a new lampshade.

Catherine had never heard of staging when a friend asked for help selling a house that had been sitting on the market for a year. "And she said, 'Do you by any chance have any furniture that you can put in this house?' I had a dining room table. Then I called up a friend and said, 'You know that white love seat in your living room? Can I borrow it?'" After Catherine worked her magic, the house sold in three days. And her phone started ringing.

Another house-selling tip: Catherine likes to let dining tables and chairs float on bare floors. "I never put rugs in dining rooms, because your eye travels to the limit of a room." A rug may be charming in your home, but a bare floor will make the room seem larger. That's one difference between decorating and staging, but not the only one.

As Catherine puts it: "The house sells, and yippee!" Then it's time to take another call. And maybe that birdcage will finally get out of storage.

Chapter Twelve

"And She Landed on Her Feet"

I f I was ever a person who needed no introduction, that time is over now, but I do make public appearances often enough to notice that lately *The Jane Pauley Show* is fading from my biography. In the interest of time? Or are people just embarrassed to mention a show that was on and off the air in less than a year. It was the hardest thing I've ever done, but I remember it as the best year of my career.

I had a theme song and a professional wardrobe, makeup, and hair team. There wasn't a star on the door, but I had a just-like-in-the-movies dressing room. It was adjacent to the studio, and I could hear the audience being loaded every day. (We weren't serving drinks. "Loading" means seating an audience.) The noisy chatter was exhilarating—everyone sounded so excited to be there—after all, they'd come to see a "show." And they gave me a standing ovation every single day. I could hear Joey, our warm-up guy, *rehearsing* this ovation, and yet my psyche responded to it as if it was totally spontaneous and sincere. Daytime TV was all new to me, but that two-armed TV talk show host wave just came naturally.

Daytime talk was a surprisingly good fit for me for many reasons. After thirty years in a relationship with a camera, I loved working with a live audience—mostly women like me. The studio audience made it more like a conversation. We talked about serious things and funny things. We had a lot to talk about, sharing stories and learning from each other. Even when things went wrong, we were in it together. The audience was totally supportive. It was good while it lasted, although it was obvious from the start that it wouldn't last long.

We hired an executive producer with a gold-plated résumé—in sports. He was game to try something new too. When the show debuted, in August 2005, my face was plastered across New York City buses for an entire month. My kids, who'd never taken much interest in my work, were finally impressed: "I saw you on the bus, Mom!"

My promotional campaign was proportionate to my competition. I was opposite Oprah in most of the country. Who could forget when everyone in Oprah's studio audience went home with a new car? That was the week my show debuted. I think our audience went home with soap. Giveaways or not, I was no Oprah. But I already knew that.

The surprise for me was that the goalposts shifted before we went on the air. Before I accepted the offer of a daytime show, I made it clear that I was interested in engaging women my age—give or take. "That's who's out there," I was assured. But the man making the assurances left the company in a management shake-up before we'd even hired a staff. New management was aiming for a new target audience—a much younger demographic—and I was not hitting it. Before the last autumn leaves dropped from the trees, several stations had dropped me into the exile of off-hour slots, which is the equivalent of cancellation. In Seattle my show aired at 1:00 a.m.—I suppose catering to the "sleepless in Seattle." But Louisville hadn't given up on me. I don't often open those binders Garry made for me, as I've been disinclined to read my own press ever since that business with the cantaloupe back in Chicago, so I only belatedly saw that the Louisville *Courier-Journal* had been more or less generous in reporting my ratings trouble. "Pauley's problem is that her show got the biggest talk-show sendoff this season, and she is failing to live up to those great expectations. If you are Tony Danza, whose show isn't doing any better than Pauley's, you don't take as much heat because you weren't in the spotlight to begin with." And some thought my show was "too cerebral—too much like NPR." I remember having a lot of fun. Our "mistake-wear" show was a blast. And after decades of being told, "I didn't know you were so *little*," what I heard most often was "I didn't know you were so *funny*."

At first I didn't know how well it *wasn't* going, but my sister did. Ann took a hiatus from her own career to come work with me as a sort of producer without portfolio. Professionally, Ann had been a leader of *men*. Her clients were men. And with a husband and two sons at home, she craved female companionship, and programmed her DVR to record Oprah, Ellen, and Dr. Phil. Ann probably knew as much about daytime TV as anyone on the staff. I could not have survived that year without her. She was widely admired and appreciated for her steady hand in a crisis, and there were many of those. About one month in, Ann attended the meeting where we were given notice that we had "six weeks to turn it around." She didn't tell me. It wouldn't have made any difference. The whole team worked as hard as hard could be worked, but we were always behind. We taped six new shows a week. The pressure was relentless. It wasn't unusual to finish the sixth show on Friday and look at the storyboard for the upcoming week—and see two or three blanks.

One Friday, when there was nothing on the board for Monday, I had an idea for a show called "Cooking 101," a concept about moms who'd forgotten to teach their grown kids how to cook. Booking a show at the last minute would have been nearly impossible, but I knew where to look.

For twenty-plus years I'd kept my family off-camera. The only published picture of my children was a shot taken by a paparazzi photographer with a long-lens camera who was stalking Garry and me when we took our twin babies for their first stroll in Central Park. But now in desperation, I called home. The kids went along with my plan, which was to pair each of them with a famous chef to prepare a dish live in the studio. But a nor'easter was rolling up the coast. There was a blizzard Monday morning.

The studio audience is more important than you know. One of the key members of a daytime talk show staff is the audience developer. Research says the home audience views the studio audience as their proxies—hence the frequent cutaways to people listening, laughing, crying. And a live audience gives a show life and energy. But with blowing snow and biting winds outside, the audience the day we taped "Cooking 101" was a no-show. We were desperate just to fill some seats. I called friends at home, we pulled colleagues out of their offices and grabbed people right off the street—mostly tourists glad to come in from the cold and happy to see a free show. Many had never heard of Jane Pauley. Quite a few didn't even speak English. Two thirds of the seats were still empty.

But our celebrity chefs—Richard Ruben, Louie Lanza, Curtis Aikens, and Marcus Samuelsson—delivered! The kids were great, too, although Tommy, almost twenty, still couldn't resist playing with the food, and when he treated a salmon disrespectfully, I said, "You're grounded!"—right on camera.

It was a fun show. And despite the writing on the wall, the ratings got better. *The Jane Pauley Show* finished as the number one new show of the season, but I wasn't surprised when it was not picked up for a second one.

I'd known from the start it would be a long shot. In fact, back when I first agreed to the show, I'd prepared my kids accordingly. And in the end, I think it was a good experience for them to see their mother try really hard and fail. Until then, as realistic role models for our children, Garry and I were ridiculous. I was on *Today* four years out of college and Garry had a contract for the comic strip *Doonesbury* when he was still *in* college.

Until the daytime show, after every bad turn my career had only veered back toward success. My departure from *Today* improbably led to the prime-time special, *Changes*, which begat *Real Life with Jane Pauley*. I got the call that *that* show was being canceled during a break in an interview with Candice Bergen, but it was a brief disappointment, as *Real Life* made way for *Dateline*.

While *The Jane Pauley Show* cancellation was not my first disappointment, it *was* a disappointment. But with my career history I had reason to expect something good to be waiting around the corner. Not this time.

About eight months after the show went off the air and a full year and a half after its big launch, one of those buses with my picture still plastered on the side suddenly reappeared.

"I saw you on the bus, Mom!" My daughter was home from school for the holidays and was standing on a street corner in New York City with a group of college friends when a city bus rolled by with my picture splayed end to end, advertising *The Jane Pauley Show*. What could it mean? Was the show coming back?

Would I be getting a call? Was it a Christmas miracle? Alas, no. The "magic bus" was never seen again.

I'm not normally prone to magical thinking, but during the final week of the show I'd had a genuinely transformational experience that turned a narrative of failure into something more positive and even empowering. It was a dream. I was a passenger in a small plane. There were two other women aboard, including my sister. Suddenly, Ann jumped out! And was quickly followed by the other woman. I didn't recall any of us having parachutes, but in a leap of faith, out I went. When I woke up, I remembered that after I touched down softly and safely, I had said to myself, "And she landed on her feet."

Chapter Thirteen

Up Periscope

I was pretty proud of that dream and enjoyed telling the story about landing on my feet, until time passed and I had to face the fact that I hadn't gotten very far. I didn't have a good answer to the question "What are you doing these days, Jane?" And after a while the question evolved into "How are you enjoying *retirement?*" I was not retired! I was *looking.*

How do you look for something when you don't know what you're looking for? Tripp Hanson told me, "For me it never happened when I was looking for it." He could have been speaking for the majority of people I've profiled in four seasons of *Your Life Calling.* While it could be said that they were "looking," most of them didn't know what they were looking for. After a career on Broadway, and in his forties, Tripp was struggling to figure out his next act. He said a therapist had suggested, "Put up your periscope. Just look around, over the fence, over the hedge, check it out. Things are going to grab your attention; pay attention when they do. When something intrigues you, pay attention. Why does that mean so much to you? Go a little further. Take it another step. Listen to that small, quiet voice."

Of all the people I've met in my *Your Life Calling* series, Tripp, with his reinvention from Broadway performer to acupuncturist, seems closest to an extreme makeover, until you ask a few questions, starting with, "What did you want to be when you grew up?"

From the age of four, Tripp wanted to be a doctor. But high school chemistry was his undoing. After the final exam ("I couldn't even understand the questions, much less the answers"), he said to himself, "Well, I could always sing." And he walked directly to the music department.

In college, Tripp studied piano and singing. Tap dancing came later. Tripp is what people in the theater call a "triple threat": he can act, sing, *and* dance. His very first Broadway show, *Crazy for You*, in 1992, was a hit. He had even appeared with the cast on *Today*.

If you ask Tripp how acupuncture came into his life, he'll tell you a story about a dog. "Spanky was my little soul mate," he says. As the story goes, his beloved dog was having trouble with his knee. Tripp lived in a two-story house, and Spanky stopped coming down the stairs. He would whine and bark and wait to be carried. Someone suggested Tripp try doggy acupuncture. And he did. After a couple visits, "bloop, bloop, bloop, bloop, bloop, bloop, bloop, bloop, bloop, right down the stairs." It worked.

With dancers, something always hurts. It just goes with the territory doing eight shows a week. Tripp was thinking, "I've had this thing with my foot. All that jumping, metal plates on the bottoms of your shoes . . . it's like being a horse, you know, your hoof goes a little funny. Maybe acupuncture would help that."

Tripp described his first visit to an acupuncturist: "He put a needle nowhere near my foot—somewhere on the side of my leg—and all of a sudden I felt this whoosh, a rush of energy. It was almost like a tiny little firecracker went off in my foot, and I was like, 'Wow, what was *that*?' My foot got better after three visits."

Still, time was taking a toll. "Forty did not feel like thirty at the end of a show. More ice, more heat, more Advil . . ." Tripp soldiered on, but he recalls thinking, "I don't want to be the fourth tap dancer from the left when I'm fifty." And there were other feelings he found hard to ignore, as he put it the day we talked. "There was a sinking, sick feeling. It's not like I *can't* do it. Maybe I don't *love* it. Love is a big thing to me. Loving what I do, feeling engaged in what I do."

A question loomed over his future: "I'm not trained for anything else; what am I going to do?"

"You were forty-two," I said. "What did you think was going to happen?"

He said, "I just kept thinking, 'I'll just keep going and things are gonna work out.'"

"That's very theater," I observed.

Tripp's transition from actor to healer was a long process. But he had that capacity Betsy McCarthy described, of being comfortable in ambiguity. "I trust destiny, I trust fate, because that's how my life has been," he explained. "I call them 'happy accidents.' For me, it never happened when I was looking for it." He hadn't been looking for a career in health care, but as his therapist had said, "When something intrigues you, pay attention." Tripp admitted, "It made me nervous the first time I saw a needle in my arm. I was a little bit like, 'Ooh, don't look at that, that's weird.' But it engaged me, and my response to it was immediate. I didn't go seek acupuncture; it got me. It came and found me." Something about acupuncture had interested him, and he listened to that voice. As Tripp described it, "bubbles" started occurring.

That description reminded me of a paragraph from *Managing Yourself for the Career You Want*, in which contributor Herminia Ibarra wrote, "People don't necessarily repress their true self; they just have multiple selves. . . . In any of us there is a part that's very pragmatic and there's a part that's very creative, and there are times in life when we give more time and space and energy to one side than to the other. But if it's in you, eventually it kind of bubbles up, and it wants some airtime."

Tripp's childhood aspiration to be a doctor bubbled back up. And acupuncture had just enough theater to it for him ("Woo Woo" is what he calls it).

I asked him why not massage, and he shot back, "Not enough

toys." He liked the toys, the theatricality of acupuncture. "We wave these little scary things called needles and people are like, 'Oh, what's that?' It suspends the Western mind. We might light some herbs and there's smoke, there's Mylar that we might cover you with to keep the heat in your body. It's shamanic."

The most roundabout stories often end up being linear when you have some perspective. Tripp found himself circling back to his earliest childhood ambition, but taking along his adult "toys" and his experience from showbiz. And not just the *show* but the *business* part.

Show business *is* a business. An actor sends out a picture, goes to auditions, makes calls to an agent or manager. Opening an acupuncture office is starting a business. But first you have to learn acupuncture. I could as easily memorize *Macbeth* as absorb the content of Tripp's acupuncture textbooks. He admits that was "the scariest part of the journey." It's complicated material, but again, his showbiz experience served him well. A dance routine is a specific set of rhythmic anatomical movements that must be learned both intellectually and physically. Tripp used his showbiz skills to learn acupuncture skills. "I'd say to myself, 'Okay, you know how to make a show, so today the show is anatomy. I would tap-dance things in my house.'"

By the way, Tripp is still in the theater. He built an acupuncture clientele of show people and makes "house" calls. His story may not inspire you to become an acupuncturist, but his insight is universal: "Reinvention happens when you realize it's not gonna happen this time unless I do it myself." That certainly resonated with me. Entering my late fifties, I knew that this time, if anything was going to happen, I'd have to make it happen myself.

I was waiting to board a plane one day and making last-minute revisions on a speech when a woman tentatively approached and apologized for interrupting me. Her name was Sue. She said she was an old fan who'd had twins, too, two years before I did. We got to talking. Sue said she and her husband had just taken a big step. They'd bought a farm.

"We're thinking, 'Oh my gosh. We don't know anything about farming,'" she said.

My laptop was open when Sue sat down, so I started taking notes. "Bought the farm"—wasn't that a euphemism for *dying*? Not to Sue and her husband. Buying the farm was a step toward the next phase of their lives. He was a doctor, not retired, but they had grown kids and she was doing a lot of thinking about the next part of her life.

"What do you want to say: 'I sat and ate lunch with people'?" She laughed, adding, "You can only play so much *golf*."

Sue and her husband didn't just buy a farm. They bought some horses—an endangered breed called Shire horses, bred to be workhorses, which I gathered were very, very large. (Sue said they could literally weigh a ton.) She explained a plan that was simmering in her mind—that these gentle giants might make good therapy animals. She was thinking about abused women. "If they could learn to be around these enormous animals, learn how to hold themselves, how to carry themselves, it might be the starting point for taking a next step."

She laughed again. "I think this is called adult ADD."

But that's how it goes. We're all entering uncharted territory. Learning from each other, looking to each other for feedback and support.

"How old are you?" I asked.

At first she said fifty-three, thought a moment, and corrected herself: "No! I'm fifty-four!" I was also fifty-four.

In television, fifty-four has special meaning. That's when a person ceases to exist. The audience demographics that are key to selling advertising time give special premium to certain categories of people. There's eighteen to twenty-five, then twenty-five to fifty-four. After that? Lately, Madison Avenue has begun to acknowledge there is life after fifty-four, but at the time, my television career had ended at the very age a woman would have entered commercial oblivion.

I told Sue I'd been thinking a lot about what to do next, too, but confessed that I was starting to worry that I'd never get around to "buying the farm," speaking metaphorically. I told her I was in a *fallow* period, which I knew was an agricultural term. Later, I looked it up.

Modern society equates lying fallow with wasting time. But lying fallow is defined as "the plowing or tilling of land, without sowing it for a season." The purpose of letting land lie fallow is to let the land replenish itself.

. . .

It had been a while since I'd checked in with Sue. The last time we exchanged emails she'd said the farm had been a "steep learning curve," but that losing her mother had been the big adjustment. When I called her recently, she said her father had moved in with her and her husband. She described a day when he wanted to make preserves. So they made preserves together that day.

It's important to remember that some of us are still raising children or looking after aging parents. Lately, many of us have grown children who've returned to the nest even while we're looking after aging parents. You've heard of the "sandwich generation." Now they're calling it a "club sandwich." Caring for so many others doesn't leave much time for thinking about yourself, much less creating a whole new you. But the time will come.

I was waiting to board another plane recently, prowling the airport newsstand for some reading. Perhaps following in my sister's footsteps, I gravitated toward business magazines. I picked up a copy of *Fast Company*. And there it was: "Sometimes the best thing a creative team should do is let an idea incubate and not rush into the next step." In other words, sometimes the best move is not to make the move, but to *incubate*. Which is not only a good piece of advice, but I recognized that incubate sounds more strategic than lying fallow. I thought about Sue and the farm. Buying the farm was a first step, but she wasn't rushing into the next step. Ideas were incubating.

Chapter Fourteen

Less THINK, More DO

There's a story I tell in my memoir about a spa vacation when a woman seeing me sitting alone in a garden (painting a watercolor) sat down beside me. She needed someone to talk to and I looked available. She told me she was recovering from an accident and was struggling to get her life back on track, but was paralyzed with indecision about what she should do next. I listened while she described three very different ideas. I told her they all seemed pretty good and suggested maybe it didn't matter which one she chose, but she might feel better if she got one of them going. I was later complimented by the wellness staff at the spa, who said my advice had been a bit of a breakthrough for her.

I may have been channeling Ronald Reagan's chief of staff. Some years ago, John Sununu and I happened to be dinner partners at an annual Washington event where journalists and politicians have fun together. Sununu was not having fun. He had no love for the media or small talk. So we sat together in rather painful silence until I asked him a question: "You must have to make a lot of big decisions every day. Do you have a strategy?" His answer was interesting. He said that in his experience most decisions can quickly be narrowed down to a couple of competing choices. And his policy was not to waste time parsing the one or two degrees of difference between them but to pick one or the other and focus one hundred percent of his energy on making it the right decision.

I'm of two minds on decisions. Little ones, like what to pack for a trip, are painful. But the big ones are easy. One of my "strengths"—so called. Marcus Buckingham and Donald O. Clifton called it "Activator." It means I'm pretty quick to pull the trigger on big decisions. This had been Garry's only quibble with my StrengthsFinder test results. "Are you sure that's a *strength*?"

As I thought about it, I realized the big decisions I'd made with such apparent ease had something in common. Each had to do with leaving. When I decide it's time to go, I start looking for the off-ramp.

For example, when my son Tom was a senior in high school and Ross and Rickie were already away at college, I began to anticipate how empty our home would feel when our family of five was down to just Garry and me. I proposed we downsize. I was surprised that Garry (who likes things to stay put) quickly gave me his blessing, but he shouldn't have been surprised at how quickly I'd make my move. Before Tom was settled in his freshman dorm, Garry and I were living in a new apartment.

Moving across town did not change the fact that several years had passed since I "landed on my feet." I was struggling to pull the trigger on the next phase of my life. Evidently, stopping is easier for me than starting. One morning I found an email in my in-box. It was from Tom.

Dear Mom,

I think that the most important thing you can do is FOLLOW THROUGH! You have lots of ideas, but it's time you really took the reins and tried to make one of them happen.

I think you've surveyed the field long enough—thinking about what might work, what you might be good at, and what you want to be doing—it's time to make your move!

It was the kind of meddling email I might have *sent* to one of my kids. I'm rather well-known in some circles for being generous with free and unsolicited advice.

Ann Kolbell, for instance. I've given her lots of advice, and she always listens patiently, then goes her own way. We have very different perspectives on life. She wades right into the details and makes her decisions deliberatively. "Reinvention" is not one of her favorite words. And she hates change.

For twenty-four years Ann was my closest associate at NBC. She knew that covering the news favored my temperament. I'm either totally in the moment or focused on the future. Our contrasting personalities were highly complementary. For twenty-four years, Ann's deliberative style kept me on task. But my decision to leave *Dateline* and sail off into the unknown left Ann adrift. I remember her asking, "Aren't you even a *little* nostalgic?"

I'm galvanized by the future, energized by change, while Ann's methodical nature is summed up in a pet phrase about "getting my ducks in a row." My sister teased her about that once, asking, "Isn't the point getting your ducks *in the water?*"

Ann is still at NBC. She dodged some bullets turning down a succession of buyout offers. But I think she's made herself too valuable for NBC to let her go.

For years, Ann and I were so linked in the corporate culture, I don't think her personal talents were always given their due. My leaving thrust her and her abilities into the foreground. But Ann surprised me recently when she said, "I'll never embrace change, but I've come to accept it." I felt humbled by the recognition that she was doing it in her own way, in her own time. She's getting her ducks lined up, but maybe they don't have to plunge into the water all at once.

Professor Herminia Ibarra has observed, "What people get wrong about reinvention is that they think they have to be *ready*. Instead, change *makes* ready." It's a bit counterintuitive, but she argues that *seeing* change happen *prepares* the brain for change. After successive rounds of buyouts, a lot of change was happening, and seeing it no doubt helped prepare Ann for change. But change happens, whether we're ready or not.

People often experience what experts call "present bias." A reference on behavioral economics in Wikipedia noted that "*now* has especially high value compared to any *future* time." I guess that's why we tend to see our future selves as strangers. It's one reason people postpone saving for retirement. In that issue of the *Harvard Business Review* devoted to reinvention, Professor Ibarra wrote about midcareer transitions: "By far the biggest mistake people make when trying to change careers is to delay taking the first step until they have settled on a destination." I think that's equally true of midlife transitions.

Ibarra advocates a counterintuitive process of *doing* first, *knowing* second. This was a reversal of some basic assumptions I'd had about reinvention. Writing my memoir was predicated on the assumption that revisiting my past might offer clues to my future. I'm ready to concede now that I was too much *think* and not enough *do*. With apologies to my friend Ann, I took my own sweet time getting *my* ducks in the water.

Have you ever watched children playing video games? They don't read instructions; they learn by doing. I remember watching my kids master Super Mario Bros. Pressing buttons at just the right moment would launch Mario into a blue void and reveal a star—rewarded by more points and more stars. Learning by doing is how they advanced through the levels.

Reinvention is a process. But I've realized that doing first and knowing second turns out to be a good description of the process that finally inspired me, as my son Tom had put it, to make my move.

Even after a career notable for the regularity with which opportunity arrived unbidden, in my mid-fifties I didn't really expect opportunity to come knocking again. I expected I would have to look for it. As Tripp Hanson put it so well, "Reinvention happens when you realize nothing is going to happen this time unless you make it happen."

I was having my hair done one day, skimming an article in *Vogue*, when something Jennifer Aniston said made my antennae quiver. It might have been all the aluminum foil in my hair, but this resonated powerfully: "Everything you want most in the world is just beyond the range of your comfort zone."

I was sinking into my comfort zone, and not just metaphorically. I knew exactly where my comfort zone was: the sofa in my living room. I spent hours there every day. I wasn't napping. It was my creative command post, my personal R & D department. (I'm sitting there now.) Given my organizational style, plowing through laptop files dated 2006 to 2009 was like wading through elephant grass, but I am frankly surprised looking back to see how busy I had been during my "fallow" period—generating ideas and testing prospective partnerships. There had been quite a lot of *doing* mixed in with all that *thinking*. I pitched multiple proposals to television executives, variations on themes of transition or reinvention. For a year and a half I worked on a prospective collaboration with PBS with the working title "How We Live." The concept was future oriented, though not futuristic. And for two years I focused on "Practical Inspiration," which was a live event with experts and exercises and audience participation—like a daytime talk show without television cameras and with a particular focus: preparing for our futures.

I collected data, quotations, and anecdotes gleaned from newspaper and magazine articles and books. Including, obviously, multiple citations from the work of Herminia Ibarra. In a recent update, she said her research has shown that the typical midcareer transition takes about three years. My own midlife reinvention took about four. In my personal experience and observation, with some of those exceptions that prove the rule, reinvention doesn't arrive as an epiphany or a single life-changing event.

Ironically, "Practical Inspiration" was my reality check. My ideas were getting some traction. There were meetings in borrowed conference rooms, and the project was on the verge of being a start-up when I realized that everyone around the conference table was looking at me as if I was the *boss*. I've been blessed with some really great bosses, but one thing I knew for sure was that I didn't want another one, but not half as much as

I didn't want to *be* one. I may have discovered my inner entrepreneur, but I don't have my sister's managerial temperament,
not to mention her skill set. I decided to strip the idea down
and take my show on the road—alone. I booked some speeches
about practical inspiration. I recognized this was not "it," but it
was a stepping-stone toward something.

Chapter Fifteen

Inspiration Is Everywhere

I asked Garry, "What's a word to describe someone who likes crossword puzzles?" He said, "Ross." I had been looking for a word to describe our son Ross's affinity for crossword puzzles. It's his favorite section of the newspaper. I don't care for the puzzles, but we subscribe to three papers. I love newspapers; they're filled with ideas. When Garry comes down for breakfast, he finds them filled with holes. I clip articles, like one with this headline: "Inspiration Is Everywhere but You Have to Be Looking." If there's a core message to be found in these pages, that's probably it.

There's no better illustration of what "looking" means than Thomas Betts. He was actively looking for that elusive *something* people have described to me so often. Remember how Tripp Hanson spoke of putting up a periscope and just looking around and if something interests you, pay attention to that? Here's how that worked for Thomas Betts.

Racing sailboats was his passion, and he'd spent many happy hours fixing up a forty-one-foot sailboat. He and his wife, Connie, had talked about sailing it around the world some day. He'd made his living designing and manufacturing equipment for sailboats. Then he sold his business. After a while, Connie suggested he needed to go back to work. He took a part-time job in sales with a company that had carried his products, and he was pretty good at it. When he was offered a management position, he took it. And he was good at that, too. He liked the people and the company and the benefits, but he didn't enjoy the stress. He was under constant pressure "to make the numbers." He heard that inner voice yearning for "something different," but that inner voice didn't say what it was.

Thomas and Connie had begun exploring the "sunny side" of the Cascade Mountains near Portland, Oregon. On weekend rambles they discovered the Fruit Loop, a thirty-five-mile stretch of country roads in the Hood River Valley. Chances are you've enjoyed cherries or apples from the valley. It's dotted with orchards and farms and ranches.

Meanwhile, back at the store one day, a customer came in to buy dock line. A lot of it. Thomas said to him, "You must have a lot of boats."

The customer said, "I don't have boats. I raise alpacas."

He can't explain why, but Thomas just had a powerful feeling that this could be "it." That night he went home and asked Connie, "What's an alpaca?"

Connie, who knitted and crocheted, knew that alpacas were bred for fiber. Alpaca yarn is some of the finest fiber in the world—very soft and warm. She had a question for Thomas: "Does he make any money at it?" They were both intrigued and began researching the alpaca business. They attended a seminar where they were told, "If you can raise a cat, you can raise an alpaca." They had cats. Good sign.

They began to think about buying property. The customer who introduced them to alpacas knew the Hood River area pretty well and found a piece of property he thought would work for them. When Thomas and Connie went to look at it, they saw run-down outbuildings surrounded by sagging fences. But the modest house was immaculate and perfect for their needs. So they sold their house in Beaverton, bought the place, and moved in.

But it wasn't an alpaca ranch yet. Thomas Betts offers a textbook example of another career prescriptive Professor Ibarra advocated, called "test and plan." He thought he might enjoy alpaca ranching, but while Connie was raised on a dairy farm, Thomas grew up with a single pet, a Chihuahua. He wisely tested the proposition before he invested in it. When the alpaca rancher gave him a chance to work part-time and learn the business, he quit his job and spent the next nine months living in the world of alpacas. "I took to alpacas 'like a duck to water,'" he told me. "It was a lot of fun. And it was easy."

It took two years and some trial and error to break even. Thomas and Connie have added other income streams to make their ranch profitable, including a yarn store on the property, which was one of Connie's dreams. They have their eye on more property, so Connie kept her job in information technology, but she's discovered a flair for marketing. She created a website, and the ranch is now a tourist destination. Cars fill the driveway on the weekends. In the store, Thomas enjoys talking about alpacas. He gives demonstrations, showing how fiber becomes yarn on a spinning wheel. He knows how to use it. He's rigged a machine that dispenses feed, so the alpacas can eat out of the children's hands.

Standing in a muddy barnyard with Thomas, wearing a pair of attractive but completely inappropriate Italian boots, I noted, "It's not necessarily a glamorous lifestyle you've chosen."

He smiled. "Well, I don't know. To me the alpacas are glamorous. I think they're beautiful. They all have personalities, and they're fun to watch in the field. They'll run and prong like deer. We'll sit on our porch and watch them play. It's entertaining. It seems like they're happy. They're very rewarding."

The most rewarding part of my job continues to be finding the improbable turns in life that take people to the most surprising places, and discovering they're not so improbable after all. Thomas already knew something about fiber because years ago he'd sold carpets. And when I asked him what his major had been in college, I was not expecting him to say music! He studied organ. The two large looms I'd noticed sitting side by side in the Bettses' house are about the same size as the organ my mother played. Like playing the organ, weaving requires both physical and mental dexterity. And another surprise was that he had worked his way through college in a machine shop. That's another income stream. He fills in at a local machine shop when they're busy. There he manufactures a metal pooper-scooper he designed and sells online. The only part of ranching he'll admit to not loving is mucking out the barn—and despite what you may read online, alpaca poop smells like poop.

There's more. After the crew packed up the gear and we were ready to leave the ranch, I learned something about Connie. She works in technology now, but she used to be a teacher. She taught high school biology, including animal husbandry. I was dizzy with all the connecting dots.

I noticed the license plates of two cars parked in the driveway: SAILING 1 and SAILING 2. But Thomas and Connie Betts have a new passion now: forty-seven of them.

While we were talking, I became aware of a sweet, low drone coming from the pen behind us in the barn. "Is that humming I hear?"

Thomas nodded. "They're talking to each other."

"What are they talking about?"

"Probably wondering what we're doing over here. They're curious. Mostly, they just hum. I think it means they're happy."

And Thomas Betts is a happy rancher.

. . .

Inspiration is everywhere. As I noted in *Skywriting*, the poet and author Rodger Kamenetz talks about "purposeful wandering," which he defines as being actively available to connections and patterns. He calls them "portals to insight." A Quaker friend (yes, I know that sounds redundant) tells me that in Quaker meetings there is a tradition called "active listening," which is intended to open the mind to insight. My friend said he thought that was another way of "looking." So is prayer. I clipped an article from the newspaper about a woman who had retired with her husband to Florida. What got my attention was that it started by saying she wasn't much of a "joiner." Nor am I. So while her husband enjoyed their new life, she was bored and looking for something to do—but more than that. She yearned for something that would give her life meaning. She prayed for insight. She prayed for a year. Until one day, she found it—on her coffee table. It was an article in a magazine about a missing child. She felt she was meant to read it. The article inspired her to create a neighborhood network of watchful eyes to protect kids. She found what she was looking for—and more. Not only does her own life have more meaning, but think of the gift she's given the hundreds of women her organization has trained, many grandmothers like herself. She's given their lives more meaning too.

I thought of Betsy McCarthy again. She had not been a joiner either. In the past, her knitting had been for her a solitary pursuit. She didn't really know any knitters. But with teaching, she said she'd become connected to knitting in a way that felt organic and historical. She thought about how women through time had gotten together in knitting circles, and while they worked with their hands they talked and developed a wonderful sense of trust. The knitting circle became like an extension of family. Betsy began to create such communities, as several knitting circles grew out of classes she taught.

One of these communities was a group of women in their seventies and eighties. "We've gone through life events with each other," Betsy told me. "Two members have had strokes. One member lost her husband. A couple are caring for husbands with Alzheimer's, and the circle is their one time away from the responsibility. People know each other. They care. People have become best friends." When you're retired, and you're in your seventies, she noted, where do you meet a best girlfriend?

But then the knitting shop where they met closed. Suddenly the group didn't have a home, and there was real fear that the circle would disband. "What's going to happen to us?" the women asked Betsy, seriously worried. That's when Betsy had her epiphany.

She found a coffeehouse that had a beautiful atrium, and Betsy told the group, "I'll be here every Tuesday I can make it, from eleven to one." They've met there for several years, and Betsy teaches that group for free. Knitting is still her passion, but she has discovered something deeper that gave her more satisfaction, and her life more meaning and purpose than knitting—

as she expressed it, "bringing people together" through teaching knitting.

When people say, "Just follow your passion," remember how Betsy found a passion deeper than the one she already knew about. And don't forget Thomas Betts. You'll recall that his passion was sailing. He still enjoys sailing, but to start his herd of alpacas, he sold his boat!

Chapter Sixteen

Work You Want to Do

I rarely miss a chance to tell this story. One summer morning, many years ago, Tom and I were standing together on the porch watching Garry and the twins build a little stone path in the garden. Rickie and Ross were busily gathering rocks and helping Daddy mix cement. I turned to Tom, who was about four, and asked if he didn't want to help. And he said, "I'm never going to do work I have to do; I'm only going to do work I *want* to do." I spent ten minutes figuring out how to punctuate his pronouncement, but several years understanding it. Tom was a little ahead of himself. When he was twenty-five, hearing me tell the story again, he asked, "What did that *mean?*" If "looking" is a core idea of this book, then "work you want to do" is the grail. Here's what it means.

Except for the lucky few, most of us spent the first phase of our working lives doing work we *had* to do. And so will Tom. But our generation is the first to realize there could be a second phase of our working lives, and that it might be different. What we're looking for is work that fits our personal needs and fulfills our wants.

Work may or may not mean a job. It may be working out a new way of living, or finding a way to be happier in your job. Remember that AARP survey in which 80 percent of baby boomers said they intended to keep on working even in retirement? Many of us will have to. But a lot of us—like Jerry Leener, who jumped at the chance to take early retirement and then worked so hard to become an *unpaid* emergency medical technician—realize that work will continue to be an important component of a balanced and fulfilling life. As Sue, who "bought the farm," said, "I mean, you can only play so much golf." Jan Erickson's husband, Jon, had sold his law practice in his fifties and was looking forward to being a fly fisherman, but as Jan put it, "I think he found out fairly soon that it lacked real meaning and purpose." She says he's thanked her many times because as partners in Janska, "he's been able to reinvent himself too." And when she said, "We think of work as play," she echoed a sentiment expressed a hundred-something years ago by Mark Twain: "The work that is really a man's own work is play and not work at all."

Many people I've interviewed who have been through midlife reinventions began with strong feelings of discontent but emerged feeling liberated and happy. On a visit to Paul Giannone (henceforth to be called Paulie) at his pizzeria, Paulie Gee's, he took me into the inner sanctum and let me watch him

make some pies. He does *not* do the standard sausage and mush-
room. His pies are wildly inventive—though he draws the line
at the letter *p*—no potato, pineapple, or pepperoni. His pies have
names like Arugula Shmoogula (Italian tomatoes, baby arugula,
olive oil, and shaved Parmigiano-Reggiano) and Still Ricotta Be
Named (fior di latte, Canadian bacon, sweet Italian fennel sausage, fresh basil, and post-oven ricotta dollops).

I told him it seemed to me he was not a dreamer but "a very methodical person with a dream." He responded, "Now I've reached
something beyond my wildest dreams." He gestured to the rustic
tables around us and the quaint sign, PAULIE GEE's. "It's hard to believe. When I was going through all those struggles in the information technology world, worried about downsizing, worried about
not being the best at what I did, I was always very nervous. But
now . . ." His voice trailed off. "I'm happy." He had tears in his eyes.

As I bit into one of his creations, he beamed. "I hope you're
enjoying it as much as I am."

It was the Greenpointer—mozzarella topped with heaps
of fresh baby arugula. It was green and white, the colors of the
Greenpoint subway stop. If you're ever in Brooklyn, drop by Paulie Gee's for some great pizza! Paul Giannone is always there. I
asked him how many days a week he worked. "Seven," he said.
Then quickly blurted out, "*No!* I work *no* days a week. I haven't
worked in over two years. I really haven't. When I come in here
I'm not working."

That, Tom, is the meaning of "work you *want* to do."

Chapter Seventeen

The Mother of Reinvention

Most of the movies inspired by the campus unrest of the sixties have not stood the test of time, probably including *The Strawberry Statement*. But it was based on a really great book written by James Kunen, then a nineteen-year-old student at Columbia. In the spring of 1978, the tenth anniversary of the Columbia student strike, I was interviewing Kunen live on *Today*, when for reasons I've never ascertained, some kid assaulted us with a cup of coffee. After that I lost track of Kunen. What became of that child of the countercultural sixties? He ended up a self-described "company man."

As director of corporate communications for Time Warner, part of Kunen's job was to reassure employees that management supported and respected them. Then, along with many coworkers, he got the pink slip. Reinvention is not always a choice.

Sometimes it's a necessity, but even necessity can be opportunity.

In his new book, *Diary of a Company Man*, he recounts being laid off along with many others in what he describes as a "brutal fashion." His reinvention is suggested by the subtitle, *Losing a Job, Finding a Life*. Today, Kunen, ex–company man, teaches English as a second language. I underlined half the book—it's hysterically funny and equally wise—and I recommend it. This is the final line: "I appreciate that there is no difference between who I am and what I am doing at last."

Which is a very good definition of that elusive concept *alignment*, and shows that "good works" and "good work" can be the same.

On the other hand, "good work" can kill you. Antoinette Little loved her job. She's a person who thrives on pressure, and as the office manager of a large law firm, she had plenty of it. She, too, came to reinvention out of necessity. She was diagnosed with a serious heart condition. While she lay on a hospital gurney, the doctors told her family, "If she doesn't quit her job, she's going to die." The stress and pressure were killing her.

Antoinette was a self-made woman. Nobody was ever going to make it happen for her but herself. The daughter of immigrants who thought *"girls"* didn't go to college, she was raised to marry and have kids—she had three daughters before she was twenty-five. She expected to be a stay-at-home mom, not a young widow. Suddenly, she had to find work. Looking in the want ads, she cannily noted that law firms paid best, so that was where she started. She found an entry-level job as a "floater" in a big law firm. Her job was to fill in whenever a legal secretary was away. She taught herself secretarial skills. Stenography? Can do! She bought books on the way home and practiced and practiced—and learned. And she made it her mission to learn everything those legal secretaries knew.

"I would go from secretary to secretary and ask them, 'Please, can I have copies of the forms, copies of what you're doing?' And I made myself a loose-leaf binder, and when an attorney would come to me and say, 'Could you do this?' I'd say, 'Oh, sure, no problem, not a problem.' Didn't know what he was talking about, but no problem. I would have to go through all my books, all my notes, all my forms, and find what was needed. If I couldn't find it, I'd go from secretary to secretary and scout around to see who did know, and then make copies of that so I could do it."

In three months she was a self-taught legal secretary. "If a managing partner or someone said to me, 'I want this done,' something inside me just couldn't say, 'I can't do it.' I had to say, 'Not a problem, I'll do it for you.'"

She rose through the ranks to executive secretary, then secretary to the managing partner, and ultimately, office administrator in a firm of sixty lawyers. She made a six-figure salary, working seventy-five, eighty hours a week, sometimes more. "I would be up at four in the morning, leave the house, start my day probably around seven a.m., work until seven thirty, eight at night, come home, bring work with me" (while being a single mother). And she was always on call when a lawyer's computer crashed or a pipe burst in the middle of the night. It was a stressful environment. But she loved being a can-do person, until the day she was told she couldn't do it anymore.

She was fifty-three when she started getting chest pains. A cardiac catheterization showed that she had an enlarged heart, a condition called "cardiomyopathy," which means heart muscle disease. The doctor stepped aside to speak with her family. He told them bluntly, "If she doesn't quit her job, she's going to die."

"What were you going to die of?" I asked her.

"I was going to die of agita, of work, of stress."

Her husband, Joe, assured the doctor, "Okay, she's quitting." Her kids agreed, "She's outta there." Antoinette is a person who lives to work. She was proud of her accomplishments. Work was her identity. She didn't know how *not* to work. But she did what she was told and quit working. At home, she did a little watercolor painting and watched a lot of QVC—and grew very depressed.

"It was like, do I have a purpose anymore?" she told me. "I wasn't bringing in the money; you feel like you have no self-worth. It's hard to describe, when you go from a position of authority and then all of a sudden, you're doing nothing."

After Antoinette's mother died and left her a little money, Joe suggested, "Why don't you go to culinary school? You love cooking. Why don't you just do it?" She said, "Well . . . maybe."

Antoinette had learned how to cook from her Sicilian father and Hungarian mother.

One day she and Joe were strolling around New York when they passed the French Culinary Institute. "Joe said, 'Let's go in,' and I said, 'Why?' and he said, 'Let's just go in and look around and see what we can do.' And we went in and found a basic pastry course, because that's what I really love doing is making pastries. And we signed up that day."

But during our interview I had a hunch that strolling by the culinary institute that day hadn't been an accident. I called out to Joe, "Was that on purpose?"

Off-camera, he called back, "Yeah!"

And Antoinette said, "You dope! You didn't tell me that."

Starting school at age fifty-three was a bit of a culture shock. "Oh, my God," she said with a laugh, "they [her classmates] were so young. Oh, my heavens, there I am with my little case and my books, and I'm walking up two flights of stairs, and mind you, I'm breathing hard. I'm gasping, and all these kids are running by me. I was the oldest one in class by at least thirty years." But she quickly discovered they looked up to her.

"Everything happens for a reason, don't you think?" she mused. "I think anybody can do anything if they put their mind to it. I'm a perfect example. You just have to have the desire and the courage to learn."

She signed up for course after course. "When you cook regular food, you can improvise—throw in a little of this and that to taste.

But when you're making a pastry, it has to be exact. It's a science." She fell in love with chocolate and is qualified now to call herself a chocolatier. She doesn't make "candy," she makes high-end chocolates. "I think I wanted to do this because it was so pretty, and I like doing things that I can be proud of, and you know if you do a pretzel, it's good. People like it. But it's not the decorative, pretty, artistic kind of chocolate."

The thing is, if something is easy, she isn't interested. "That's strange, isn't it?" she asked. It's just Antoinette.

A not-so-easy idea—opening a chocolate shop—began to take shape in her mind. But they don't teach you how to do that in culinary school. She did her homework—running the numbers, scouting locations—with her typical tenacity. Antoinette is not too quick to pull the trigger on big decisions. "Besides following your heart and not being afraid to fail, you have to do it smart," she told me. "Don't just jump into it and think, 'Okay, I want this, so it'll work.' Make sure there's a need for what you're doing in the area."

Antoinette and Joe fell in love with historic Phillipsburg, New Jersey, a quaint tourist town a half an hour from the Poconos, halfway between Philadelphia and New York City. They bought an old building loaded with charm (meaning it needed lots of work) and hung out a sign: ANTOINETTE CHOCOLATIER.

She still works long hours. Chocolate is a seasonal thing. People eat ice cream, not chocolate, during the summer, but during the Christmas season she might work from seven a.m. to midnight seven days a week. She goes home tired. "But it's a different tired. It's not a stressful tired. It's a labor of love, it's a tired that you feel like you've accomplished something fun. There's pressure, but it's a different kind of pressure. I put the pressure on myself. I don't have sixty attorneys putting pressure on me in addition to what I put on myself." Not to say she wouldn't go back in a heartbeat—if she could. "I loved it, and I still miss it." But she's filled in the missing parts. She found purpose, personal identity, and a feeling of accomplishment.

The money? Five years in, she was only just in the black—meaning she had stopped *losing* money. She expected that. "From what I've read, it takes a good five years before you can give yourself a paycheck, so make sure you've got some other money supporting you—thank you, Joe!" But now that her children are grown, Antoinette isn't in it for the money. "I'm in it for the love. I'm in it for the smiles. I'm in it for the kids coming in. I'm the favorite aunt now."

She says her proudest moment was making Molly's Truffle, named after her mother. "She left me the money to go to culinary school, and that was the very first chocolate I made, and I called it a Molly—and I topped it with twenty-three-karat edible gold, because she was such a jewel to me." Her mother's picture hangs in Antoinette's kitchen. "She watches me cook." The Molly is her bestseller.

Antoinette invited me into her kitchen. We put on white aprons and caps, and she talked about making truffles as we melted and stirred the chocolate. "It's almost like a Zen feeling," she said. "It sounds weird, but it's almost spiritual. It's warm, it's silky, it's just soothing."

Antoinette is healthier now. "The heart is a muscle," she explained, "and just like any muscle in the body, it can strengthen, and my heart has gotten stronger, so it's in good shape. I'm not perfect, but it's in good shape."

I always believed in chocolate therapy.

I don't think Mary Reed was a born leader. It was just one of the things she learned along the way. Leadership is the defining feature of her career and of her life.

After getting a master's degree forty years ago, Mary aspired to run a community program, which she did—and then a larger one, and a larger one—but not by dint of personal ambition. Mary's leadership and management skills were usually recognized a little before she recognized them herself—such as her promotion at the YWCA. "I remember going down to the main branch," she recalled, "and everyone was looking like a disaster had struck. I was pulled aside by the person I reported to, who said, 'You know, the director has been let go.' I was panicked thinking about saving my program if the director was gone."

But the board already had a replacement in mind. It was Mary! At first, she was afraid, and said no, but then she said yes, and Mary became the first African-American director of the Boston YWCA—which, by the way, was the first YWCA in

America. In Mary's career path, opportunity seemed always to be waiting just around the bend, catching her by surprise before she thought she was ready. But in the end, she always said yes, figuring that whatever she didn't know she would learn.

Her career continued to rise in stature and influence. Out of the blue, she got a call from one of the biggest search firms in Boston. Goodwill was looking for an executive vice president. She was told, "They've interviewed a ton of people and your name keeps coming up." The job would mean managing a budget three times bigger than the Y's. As if trying to talk her out of the job offer, she told the CEO, "I don't know anything about your core programs for people with disabilities." The CEO responded, "Everything you've done shows that you probably can learn."

But at the age of fifty-eight, at the pinnacle of her career, Mary's path took a sharp turn. It wasn't opportunity this time but obligation. When her mother died, Mary's reinvention began. Hearing her mother's life calling, she found her own.

Bessie Tartt Wilson was a force of nature. Generations of Bostonians sent their children to Tartt's, the nursery school program she created. It was a family business. Of her youth Mary said, "I always felt I was working, doing something to help out. You know, even when we were little, when she picked up children, I was the bus monitor in the car." A little introverted by nature, Mary credits working in the school with helping her develop people skills, through her relationships with the nursery school parents. She came to realize that she was not only "good with people" (I can attest to that!) but enjoyed it.

Her mother was trained as a nurse, and taking care of babies and little ones seemed very natural to her. But Mary described her mother's innate sense of business. "It was a pay-as-you-go operation," she said, laughing as she remembered how her mother accepted weekly payments "tucking the cash in her bosom. That would be the bank until we got home." In her later years, Bessie would turn to Mary for help with the books, but she ran the business until the Friday before her death at the age of seventy-two.

And then Mary told me, "Everybody in the family looked to me." What would happen to the family business now? "My mother put years of hard work into building something. Was I going to walk away?" She couldn't say no. Even though she'd spent years building a career of her own, she stepped into her mother's shoes. But child care had changed since the early days when Tartt's Day Care served working-class families in the Roxbury area of Boston.

The new clientele were families working hard just to keep ahead of poverty. Mary stepped back into an entirely new world. When she crunched the numbers, it was clear that the business was unsustainable financially. But she also realized that the state's child-care model was unsustainable for children. If a parent lost a job or got in trouble, by law state child-care aid stopped. The school lost the tuition, and the child simply vanished from the rolls. Mary called around and found it was happening in many other child-care programs. Thinking about all those "missing kids"—that's when Mary Reed's reinvention *really* began. Mary applied her own know-how and people skills not only to carrying on her mother's work and saving the family business, but also to pursuing the *mission*.

Her mother had been a child-care innovator, who aspired to prepare her little ones to succeed in kindergarten and believed that early education was the key to succeeding in life. But Mary understood that the opposite is also true. The seeds of poverty are planted early in life. Mary didn't have to explain to me the meaning of the "cradle to prison" pipeline. In my own advocacy work, I've learned that poor elementary school attendance and reading proficiency levels have been used by policymakers for decades as benchmarks for future incarceration.

Lobbying the Massachusetts legislature, Mary got the law changed so that children of parents who fell behind or messed up would not suffer disruption in early education. She was selected as a Purpose Prize fellow for her work as an advocate for early education under the auspices of the Bessie Tartt Wilson Initiative for Children.

Carrying on her mother's work has given purpose to Mary's life. Now in her seventies, she's still working. When we talked, Mary was six years beyond the so-called retirement age. "My children keep reminding me, 'You keep saying you're going to stay home more and work in your garden and you're going to travel more,'" she told me. "But it's like, 'Okay, I'm going to get to that.' But I really don't want to. It makes me feel alive to do this work."

Chapter Eighteen

Epiphanies Happen

One of the joys of an empty nest is reading the paper together on a quiet Saturday morning. "Look at this," Richard Bowen said, pushing the morning newspaper toward his wife, Jenny. It was a photograph—a little girl in a crib who appeared to be starving to death. The accompanying story was about a documentary shot undercover in China called *The Dying Rooms*. Richard and Jenny read about baby girls abandoned just because they were girls. With China's one-child policy, giving birth to a girl was considered unlucky; it was common for these children to be discarded to give people a chance to try again for a boy. It was estimated that since the one-child policy was established, in 1979, 15 million girl babies had been abandoned.

Reading the story, the Bowens felt compelled to *do* something. Richard said, "We could bring one home." Jenny replied,

"Yes, let's do that." Just like that. After Richard left for work, she spent the rest of the day on research.

Research was something Jenny excelled at. "I started poking around on the Internet"—which most of us weren't doing yet in 1996. "I started reading more about China and about orphans in China." The Bowens had raised a family already, with two grown daughters, but they'd started young and weren't yet fifty. At the end of the day, Richard asked Jenny to meet him at their favorite Chinese restaurant. She arrived with a fat binder full of information about orphan girls in China, and how to go about adopting one. They were committed.

After a long adoption process, the Bowens went to China to meet the baby girl who would be their daughter. They were shocked by what they saw: rows and rows of cribs, sometimes two or three babies to a crib. Two thousand children in that single orphanage, with untrained caregivers so overwhelmed that it was all they could do to feed the babies and change their diapers. Equally shocking was what they heard: silence. "Rooms and rooms full of babies, newborns, a year old, eighteen months old, not crying," Jenny said. "You walk into any other place with three babies and at least one of them will be crying. But babies cry because they know that's the way they get what they need. Babies in these orphanages quickly learn that crying doesn't get them anything."

When her daughter, Maya, was placed in her arms, Jenny experienced a surge of maternal emotion but felt absolutely nothing coming back. Maya, she says, "was emotionally vacant. She was blank. She had a flat affect. And when we got her back to the hotel room, and put her down, she couldn't walk. She was almost two years old and she had no language, because no one had ever talked to her."

They were told that Maya had been left on a pedestrian overpass in front of a bus station and was brought to the orphanage when she was about a year old. As a mother myself, I had to stop and think about that, and I said to Jenny, "Someone gave her up after a year. That would be really hard."

Jenny replied with compassion, "I can only speculate that the person who left that baby waited long enough to see that someone picked her up and took her. It can't have been done cavalierly. I know now that a lot of mothers are forced to do so by other family members."

The Bowens didn't know what to expect when they brought Maya home to San Francisco. But Jenny observed, "Maybe the most beautiful thing about bringing a new child into your life when you're fifty years old is that you don't put all those expectations on your child. I felt that she was meant to be my daughter, and whatever she became would be okay. I just wanted her to be happy."

The Bowens made Maya the center of their busy lives. Richard is a cinematographer. Jenny, a filmmaker and screenwriter, was cutting a movie at the time. "I brought the editor and the assistant editor to my home. We set up a room in the house as the editing room, and Maya sat on my lap for six months." Jenny never put her down. Maya's first words were lines of dialogue from a courtroom scene. "It was something like, 'He didn't do it!' The whole room fell apart laughing." Maya, of course, didn't know what the words meant, but to Jenny the meaning was clear: "There's a little person, and she's working."

On the Fourth of July, about a year after the Bowens brought Maya home, this story became something more profound than a heartwarming tale. They were having a backyard party. Jenny glanced out her kitchen window and had a life-changing epiphany. "I saw my little girl romping around in the garden, calling out to her friends, full of life, singing, so full of joy and happiness. In that moment, through the kitchen glass, maybe because I was a filmmaker, I saw a child who looked like she had been adored from the moment she was born. Then I got it."

Richard recalled that Jenny told him, "I know what I'm going to do with the rest of my life." Jenny doesn't remember that, but vividly remembers in that moment of clarity recognizing "that what we had given her by having her on my lap constantly, by talking to her in her face all the time, never letting her out of our sight, you know, just loving her up—that was all that little girl needed. And that must be what all of them need. Why don't we just do that for all the kids we can't bring home?"

How would she accomplish that? "Every child needs a family," she replied. "I might be able to bring the feeling of family into the lives of children in institutions by finding people who would come in and work with these babies and toddlers and pre-schoolers, and be kind of surrogate parents, people to love those children, to hold them, to make them feel like their lives matter."

How would she accomplish *that*? China is not famously open to foreign ideas. Nor was Jenny an expert on child development. She had no more background in policy and diplomacy than you or I have, wasn't wealthy, and didn't speak Chinese.

She had to find experts, partners, and resources. The parents of other adopted daughters from China rallied behind her and have been her strongest allies. Her career gave way to her vision, and her vision became Half the Sky Foundation, named after a Chinese proverb, "Women hold up half the sky."

When Jenny finally had her chance to go to China in 2000, this is what she said to authorities there: "We are so grateful for these beautiful children in our lives, and we want to work with you as a partner to give a gift back to the children who remain in the institutions. Will you let us work with you to try and bring the love of family to children who don't have families?"

The sensitivity of her appeal worked a small wonder. Half the Sky was given permission to set up two small pilot programs—for one year. They began recruiting nannies, or "zumas," which is Chinese for grandma. Hundreds of women applied. Thirty were chosen. "It was all casting. You see it in their eyes, you talk to them about children, you either see a sparkle or you don't," Jenny said. American experts trained the zumas in child care and nurturing skills, and gave them children to care for. The results were striking. "Within six months, they were behaving like children. They attached to their caregivers, they started making eye contact, looking into the eyes of their nannies and their teachers." Study groups were dispatched from Beijing to see what the Americans were doing.

It has been painstaking work. There is no fast-forward in real life, but Half the Sky has scaled up a thousandfold. There are programs in over fifty Chinese institutions. And in 2011 the Chinese government announced its commitment to make Half the Sky's programs available to every orphaned child in the nation. Jenny Bowen is so revered there that when the Olympic torch was carried to Beijing, she was given the honor of being one of the torchbearers.

Jenny goes to China every couple months. She works very, very hard but feels very lucky. "How many people can wake up every morning knowing that they're doing something to make people's lives better? Especially children's lives, innocent children who did nothing to deserve the horrible hand that fate has dealt them. I would have been an idiot not to do this."

Jenny no longer writes screenplays, but she's written a new narrative for tens of thousands—maybe hundreds of thousands—of abandoned children, weaving tender, loving care into their lives. Maya, meanwhile, has grown into a bright and beautiful teenager—with a bright and beautiful little sister. The Bowens adopted Anya three years after Maya. When I visited their home, the girls prepared a Chinese "hot pot" for me. Maya chopped vegetables, and Anya helped me create a spicy dipping sauce that suited my midwestern tastes. It was all delicious.

As I said before, usually when I do an interview, I can't help but try to connect the dots. Sometimes it's easy. Gid Pool's journey from class clown to stand-up comic was not a straight line, with all those zigs and zags in between, but I thought I could see the logic in it: a salesman confident in his personal impact on people, resilient when he didn't make the sale, and ever ready to try something new. Gid's "dots" lit up for me as clearly as a string of Christmas lights. But as Jenny Bowen told me her epic story, she seemed as regular a person as you or me. From mother and filmmaker to world changer. I couldn't connect the dots. Until she connected them for me. She explained: "I think everything that Half the Sky is I learned as a filmmaker. I start with a blank piece of paper. I have an idea, I write a story, I cast it, I find a location. I know how I want it to end. I dream a world that doesn't exist, and I find a way to get there."

Jenny has found a Chinese quotation from 500 A.D. that says, "All the children who are held and loved will know how to love others. Spread these virtues through the world, nothing more need be done."

By definition, an epiphany is a sudden revelation. When Jenny Bowen looked out her kitchen window that fateful afternoon, did the idea suddenly come to her, or had it been incubating for a while? I can only wonder. But Ken Wood's epiphany arrived completely and utterly out of the blue when an improbable delegation pulled into the driveway to look at a drilling rig he'd advertised for sale.

Some early hardships had paved the way. Ken told me he had always figured he'd go to college, and maybe follow a profession like law. But when the time came, there was no money for college. Being a farm boy in rural Maryland, he looked around for something to do and found a local well-drilling business, learned the trade, and started a business of his own.

Making a living drilling wells is hard work, and it took a toll. Ken had had two major heart attacks before he was sixty (though it's hard to fathom as he bears a robust resemblance to Clint Eastwood). He was looking forward to turning the company over to his kids and retiring. He'd enjoy his classic car collection and his stable of harness racing horses.

He was definitely *not* looking for reinvention. Reinvention found him. It was serendipitous, surprising, and transformational. A drilling rig is a big piece of machinery on wheels. A church delegation from a small town in Pennsylvania came to look at the one Ken had for sale. They were a little surprised by the price—about $75,000. Ken offered to knock a big chunk off the cost, but they left to think it over.

The second time they came back with a request. Would Ken lend them the rig, and set it up in their town where people could see what they were trying to raise money for? They wanted to drill wells in Ghana, West Africa, where people were dying from drinking putrid water. He agreed. Once they raised the money and owned the rig, they asked Ken if he'd come to Africa and show them how to use it. He was very busy. "Maybe," he said, but it felt more like no.

Two weeks later, he attended a bank seminar where by weird coincidence the keynote speaker was a man from Ghana who talked about the desperate need for freshwater wells. "It scared the bejesus out of me," Ken said, "like God's talking to you, you know." Ken is a religious man.

He went home and told his wife he was going to Ghana.

Ken was brought to a village water hole. "It was a scum pond," he told me, "a little four-foot round puddle, and they would come and squish the scum off the top of this green water and fill their jugs. There wasn't enough water even to wash. They just kept that for drinking, and you would not let your dog touch the water, it's that bad."

Ken had never been keen on traveling, but after he drilled the first well in Ghana, he knew this was going to be the first of many trips. "I would watch these people, with tears coming out of my eyes. It's devastating. I thought, suppose you have a friend that is sick all the time and you could do something . . . just click your fingers and do something to heal that person. I could do that for a thousand people a day, maybe two thousand. That's the greatest gift in the world."

Ken has since drilled more than one thousand wells in Africa—on his own and at his own expense. He sold the car collection, but not his horses. What they win at the track goes into wells in Africa. Ken can't explain it, but he says that when he's in Africa, his horses win.

While he's saving lives, he's transforming others. Most of his family and many friends, including one of his partners in the horse business, have joined drilling expeditions. Ken described the partner's experience: "He was extremely nervous, taking Paxil for his nerves. His business was driving him crazy, but when he came back, he'd lost thirty pounds, he threw the pills away, and his wife says I brought a new man back. It just changed his perspective on life—things he thought were so important are not as important as he thought they were. I wish I could take everyone there. It just changes your outlook."

Ken is thankful now that he didn't become a lawyer. Working with his skilled hands, he's saved more lives than if he'd gone to medical school and become a doctor. In Ghana he's been given a tribal name which translates as Chief Living Water, and people pray he'll live a long life because he's saving so many.

Chapter Nineteen

One Step at a Time

I heard an echo of Steve Jobs's "You have to trust that the dots will somehow connect in your future" when Joe Liles told me what he'd learned hiking the Appalachian Trail. "What I found is you can't look at the big picture. The big picture is too big. You've got to take that first step, and then in many cases, the next step will be revealed to you, and you take that step, and the next step will be revealed. You have to have faith that those next steps will be revealed."

It's said that a journey of a thousand miles begins with a single step. Joe Liles went on a journey of discovery twice as long. "They say that on the Appalachian Trail there are five million steps," Joe told me. He hiked every one—2,200 miles—and the trail changed him. Joe wasn't looking for a new life; he was looking "for a new way to live."

Joe was an unhappy man. "I kind of felt like I was doomed to live life the hard way," he told me. "Everything was gonna be difficult. It got so ridiculous that I thought traffic lights were conspiring against me—when they saw me coming, they changed from green to yellow to red." His eleven-year-old daughter told him, "This is not healthy."

Joe was not an outdoorsman by nature, though as an art teacher in North Carolina, he often took his classes outside to be inspired by the natural world. When he was forty-seven, Joe and his daughter went hiking on a piece of the Appalachian Trail. Along the way they encountered "thru-hikers"—people who were hiking the entire trail, from Georgia to Maine. "They were so friendly, so enthusiastic, so full of energy," he said. "They had a light in their eyes that I had never seen before, and I wanted to find that light for myself." Most thru-hikers are two or three decades younger than Joe, but he was enthralled by the idea. "It would be like a new chapter. I could start over with things. I could maybe reprioritize things."

Joe was not one to just ditch his job and take off. It would be a dozen years before he set off on the trail. He calculated that at age fifty-eight he would be able to retire with a pension; then he would prepare for a year and hike the trail when he was fifty-nine. But the trail was already starting to change him. Just having a goal—even a really long-term goal—was transformational.

He began preparing himself, mentally and physically. He

learned as much as he could about the trail and the provisions and gear he'd need. He figured out how he was going to handle the many logistical and physical challenges. "While I was still teaching, there was one stairwell at my school that was just four stories tall, but I ran up and down that stairwell all the time. The students must have thought I was crazy."

And he trained at the Eno River State Park. "Other hikers would laugh at this; the tallest elevation out there was maybe three hundred feet. But I did Cox Mountain over and over again. At first, I couldn't make it up halfway without stopping and panting, and then I could." He trained for camping in cold weather. "Any time the temperature in North Carolina would go below freezing, I was out there camping at the wilderness campsite just to prove to myself that I could be comfortable in cold weather."

As planned, he retired in the spring of 2008 and spent a year organizing the trip. A thru-hike typically takes six months. He packed preaddressed boxes filled with provisions and prepared a schedule for their delivery at points along the way. On March 9, 2009, at age fifty-nine, Joe set off—into three straight days of rain.

Despite all his preparation, he was afraid. "I was petrified of spending the night alone in the wilderness," he told me, adding that one is never truly *alone* in the wilderness. "I was convinced that bears were going to come and eat me—that was part of my conspiracy-type thinking." Most nights he shared shelters along the trail with other hikers. His first night as a solo camper happened by accident in Virginia, on top of Audie Murphy mountain, named for the most decorated fighter pilot in World War II, who crashed and died there after the war. "I climbed that mountain; I went to his memorial and paid my respects," Joe recalled, "but it was so far to the next shelter. As night started to fall, I realized I was going to have to camp up there on this mountain by myself. I pitched my tent and had one of the best camping experiences I've ever had in my life. When I woke the next morning and I was still alive, I realized I could do that again, and the worst-case scenario would not happen to me." His outlook on life was subtly changing.

"It wasn't an immediate transformation," Joe was quick to add. "I can remember one time—the rain had stopped, the sky was blue. I was just merrily hiking along, and all of a sudden I felt rain. I looked up and there was a black cloud right over me. It didn't just sprinkle, it poured. I am ashamed to admit this, but I cursed Mother Nature. Now, Mother Nature forgave me for that, and as soon as I started recognizing the trail as my ally instead of my enemy, things started to change for me."

Joe learned to find the humor in everything. Like the time he slipped and fell facefirst into the mud, pinned down by the weight of his backpack. "When I got up, my glasses were completely covered with mud, and my first reaction was, 'I can't see! I've gone blind!' and then I took off my glasses and I just started laughing."

There really are bears in the wilderness. The Appalachian

Trail Conservancy website warns, "While attacks on humans are rare . . . if you are actually attacked by a bear, you should fight for all you are worth with anything at hand—rocks, sticks, fists." Joe thought about bears a lot.

"At first I was afraid of seeing bears, and then after a while, I lost that obsessive fear and I actually *wanted* to see bears," he said. "I knew I would see 'em in the Smokies. Well, everybody else but me saw bears in the Smokies. Then I knew I was gonna see 'em in the Shenandoahs, and everybody but me saw bears. And then I came into New Jersey. One noontime eating lunch—a bagel with peanut butter for protein and cheddar cheese and honey—I felt something watching me, and I turned my head and there was about a two-hundred-pound bear sittin' maybe fifty yards away watching every bite that I was taking. As soon as I turned my head and he realized that I knew he was there, he bounded off through the woods. It really amazed me that he did not make one sound."

Swapping stories is part of the culture of the trail. As are trail names. Joe went by Braid, because he wears his long hair in a braid. He came to know many others by their trail names—Cruiser and Old Goat, and Check Six, and Oh Gee, Prairie Dog, and Floater (who gained his name after almost being washed away in his tent during a Georgia storm). To this day Joe knows very few of their real names.

On the trail Joe found community, and the meaning of what hikers call "trail magic": "In a literal sense, trail magic is the kind things people do for you. It could be a stranger in a parking lot handing out Snickers bars, it could be someone offering you a shower and a place to stay in their home while you're on the way. But trail magic can almost be like a state of mind. Once you believe in the positive force of life, more of these magical occurrences, opportunities, and good deeds come to you. And my life after the trail has taught me that."

Joe left for his journey a pessimist and returned ready to face his future with confidence and optimism. "It was harder than anything I'd ever experienced, but I found out what getting up every morning and hiking fifteen or twenty miles can do for you," he said. "If I can focus that kind of energy on the things that I care about, I can do some amazing things with this next chapter of my life."

Moving into uncertainty involves managing risk—planning, preparing, practicing—like Joe did before he took his first step on the trail. But even then, as Joe put it, "nothing can prepare you for the trail like getting out there on the trail and just doing it."

When Joe hiked the Appalachian Trail, he climbed mountains ("followed by more mountains"), crossed rivers and streams, and traversed boulder fields that could stretch for miles. "Sometimes," he said, "you would find the spots between the boulders I called the 'grounded path.' It was a safe path to take. If you fell, you weren't going to fall far. But there was also another path that was kind of like over the top." That one he called the "above the earth path." It was faster than the grounded path, but there was more risk to it. "I found that you had to kind of mix it up. There were times you had to pay attention to your body and your mind and you took that safer path, and then there were times you knew you could take the path that was more risky and you would be okay. I think there are times in life like that too. But the trick is knowing the difference between when you should take the grounded path and when you should take the above-the-earth path."

Since Joe returned from the trail, he has immersed himself in Native American culture, especially music. He formed a band called Braid & the Hiker Trash, performing hikers' songs. And he wrote a book about his experience, called *Trail Magic: Reports from Braid*. "I love telling stories, I love the chance to inspire people, and I'm hoping that will only continue with more intensity in this last chapter of my life."

As I sat with Joe at the foot of a rock wall at Bear Mountain State Park, where the trail cuts through New York, he offered to brew me a cup of tea on his campstove. It was a contemplative scene, though we were being filmed by a camera crew and I was on the lookout for bears.

"Joe," I said, "when you're out here in the wilderness, the idea of what you're going to do next doesn't seem very pressing."

"That's true, but, Jane, there's a saying on the Appalachian Trail: 'The trail will provide.' So you don't have to worry about what comes next, the trail will provide."

"A metaphor for life?"

"Absolutely."

No longer "doomed to live life the hard way," Joe Liles is emblematic of the power—good or bad—of the stories we tell about ourselves.

If the Appalachian Trail is the beginning, skid row is the end of the line.

The Midnight Mission in Los Angeles is at the end of skid row. You'll know you're in the neighborhood when tents and boxes begin to line the sidewalks. People live in them. Orlando Ward lived in a box for a while. He was known as Slim. It wasn't like adopting a "trail name." By that time he'd completely given up his sense of personal identity, including his name. His address? "*I* was my address."

Once upon a time Orlando was going places. He went to Stanford, was recruited as a talented basketball player until an injury ended his playing days. The descent into drugs didn't start right away. He got an education. And had some good jobs. But then, "Happy hour became happy couple of hours, happy night, happy couple of days. Somewhere during that period I crossed that invisible line where it was no longer recreational and I had become an addict, an alcoholic. And I kept going into darker and deeper and darker places." That began a pattern that carried on for the next seventeen years: "Get somewhere, build a wonderful structure of success, and just tear it all down piece by piece, whether it's jobs or relationships."

There were many years of drugs and denial. Orlando sought help, over and over. He's been in rehab maybe a dozen times. "It became my summer vacation, you know," he said. "I'd go in for sixty days, ninety days, maybe even for six months."

"The people who loved you, did they finally cut you off?" I asked him.

"Yeah. I remember I called my mom one day. I had put together some story about needing money again. And it was the most shocking short sentence my mom has ever said to me. It was, 'Orlando, I don't know what you're doing, I didn't raise you that way, but I can't help.' And she hung up."

Seventeen years after Stanford, he just let go. He was living in the box. "I'm drinking, but it's having no effect. I can't get a high anymore. I don't know where the impulse came from, but I just started to talk to God. And I just thanked Him for the wonderful parents and all the opportunities and everything that I had seen in my life. I acknowledged, I am an addict, I'm an alcoholic, I'm here on skid row and I'll probably die here. I was okay with that. The fight was gone. I had given up. I had surrendered, which was the first step in turning my life around."

"You weren't forty years old," I said.

I met Orlando at the Midnight Mission, where he began to rebuild a life, in fits and starts. He remembers thinking as he surveyed the place, "These people don't know what they're doing. I should be running this place. I figured I had a lot of experience with rehab, so I think I can run one now."

He was a client at the mission for a couple months. A client has to earn the privilege of a job. Orlando started working in the dining room, which serves 750 to 1,000 people per meal. "The line used to wrap all the way around the building. So it was a hectic, fast-paced kind of thing, and easy to get in a production mentality: 'No, you can't get extra this, you can't get extra that.'"

One morning Orlando and his "bunkie"—the guy in the next bunk—had an idea. "I don't know who said it first, me or him, that we were gonna make the Midnight Mission dining room the Nordstrom's of dining rooms on skid row," he said. "So we got up, we ironed our shirts, ironed our pants. We got new hats, we put them on, and we went in to our jobs, not as something we needed to do but as an opportunity to help somebody."

People noticed the change in Orlando before he noticed it himself. He got a promotion to the stockroom. One day a member of the executive staff found him at a computer creating an Excel spreadsheet to organize the inventory. She said, "Who are you?" Nobody knew his story. The next day she asked if he'd thought about being an administrative assistant. There was an opening—typing and filing. When he started editing a fund-raising letter, she asked, "What's your background?"

"I still was not ready for full disclosure," he said. He didn't tell her he'd gone to Stanford. I asked if it made him feel bad.

"Yeah, because I wasn't living up to it. I wasn't creating the next Google or Yahoo. It was painful."

Orlando takes the cliché out of the school of hard knocks. He's learned the hard way, as he put it, that "the stories we tell ourselves can be the wind under our wings and allow us to soar, or they can be a cage that locks us in. Our real quest is to write another story."

I met Orlando twelve and a half years of sobriety later. "I spent over a decade of my life with the Midnight Mission, as a client, as an employee, as a supervisor, as a manager, as an executive vice president of operations," he said, counting off the steps to his reinvention. He has the distinction of being the highest-ranking executive at the Midnight Mission to come up off the street.

But he recently left the mission to take on a bigger assignment as the director of community affairs at Volunteers of America, Los Angeles. Everyone knows his story now. "I think I have a responsibility to demonstrate to people who are where I was that there are no limits—none," he said. Orlando has a lovely wife and a handsome young son. And in the end, he made his mom and dad really proud.

He says he's in the "hope business."

Chapter Twenty

Spirit of Adventure

Trudy Lundgren, a graphic designer, was fifty-five when she decided to make every day a new adventure and literally make the highway her home. Trudy and her partner, Lisa, shared a cozy five-hundred-square-foot apartment in New York City when the September 11 attacks happened. September 11 came as a tremendous emotional shock, but it was also a blow to Trudy's business, since many of her clients were in downtown Manhattan. "My business tanked. Every month my income was going lower and lower and lower, and the realization dawned that I couldn't afford to live in the city anymore. So Lisa and I got out."

Trudy was quick to add they weren't running away. Some of her best memories were on the road. When she was in high school, her family moved from Los Angeles to Washington, D.C., and drove across the country, pulling a little fifteen-foot travel trailer. It took a month and a half, and it was one of the happiest times of her childhood. Buying an RV and living on the road had been something Trudy and Lisa had considered doing "one day." That day just came sooner than expected. "We upped the timetable about ten years." And to be accurate, their "home" is not an RV. The Catbird Seat is a bus, a vintage Blue Bird Wanderlodge.

For six years, it's been their 320-square-foot home-office, but it's not a never-ending vacation. They set out without a plan, figuring they'd pick up whatever work they could find. "Work camping," for instance, means living in RV parks for free in exchange for doing odd jobs on the site—yard work, office work, cleaning bathrooms, cleaning pools ("the best tan I'd ever had in my life"). Trudy cashiered at Wal-Mart. Lisa was a hotel maid and worked at McDonald's.

"And you left New York for *that*?" I had to ask.

"After having a career of sitting behind a desk all day long and working on a computer, it was a nice change of pace to do physical work," Trudy said. "It was freeing for the mind and it was different. Less responsibility, less hassle. It was a good thing."

But they still had bills to pay. The bus gets six or seven miles a gallon—"with a tailwind downhill." A fill-up is a quick two hundred dollars. The reality checks kept coming. A new engine—that was twenty thousand dollars. And housework has a special meaning when your home is a bus. "But the good far outweighs the bad, and the good adventures, the people you meet, experiences that you have are well worth dealing with your own sewage," Trudy said.

The biggest and happiest surprise was the community they found on the road. "We've met people from bikers to executives, from younger to older, from uneducated to Ph.D.s." "RV" is a verb in that community, and people from all walks of life are doing it. "It's not so much where you come from or what you do that's a determining factor. I think it's more about attitude—about being an adventurous person. RVers are resourceful. Stuff happens, and you can sit around and cry over it, or you can just get on with your life."

Trudy and Lisa abound in resourcefulness. And they hit upon a clever business model—designing brochures for RV campgrounds. Lisa sells local ads and Trudy does the graphics. "Look at the view out my office, and every couple of weeks it changes," she said enthusiastically. I wondered, though, if at some point there would be—metaphorically and maybe literally—an end to the road.

"There's a place in Texas called the Care Center, and it's for people who are RVers that can't RV anymore," Trudy explained. "They call it 'hanging up your keys.' You park your rig permanently and live there. There's a day-care center where they feed you, they do your laundry and they clean your rig." It was kind of an appealing idea—like a happy hunting ground for RVers. Trudy figured it would be quite some time before she hung up her keys.

The story of Trudy and Lisa living the RV life has been the most viewed *Your Life Calling* segment on the AARP website (www.aarp.org). Seeing the USA—from the comfort of your own living room—seems to have struck a chord. I enjoy moving furniture, but I like the room to stay put. I'm not an adventure seeker.

My husband grew up in the Adirondack Mountains, literally down the road from a ski hill. He could hike up after dinner and have a few runs. I grew up in Indianapolis. Our driveway had a bit of a slope, so getting to the school bus on a wintry morning could sometimes be a slip and a slide, but I never put on skis until I had kids. In the spirit of demonstrating that Mommy could face fears and try new challenges, I signed up for three lessons. Having never ridden a ski lift before, it came as a shock that there was nobody waiting at the top to help you off, like a ride at Disney World. And not only is the icy ground still several feet below, but you're expected to leap off and glide away on those slivery sticks— or be crushed by an oncoming gondola. All I learned after three lessons was that I'd miscalculated the magnitude of my fears. My children would just have to face theirs some other way.

I'm also scared of horses and other large domesticated animals. On my grandparents' farm, the cheeping chicks and kittens were fine, but Daisy the cow, with her lazy big brown eyes and fluttering eyelashes, was terrifying. We took a neighbor boy down to the farm one Sunday and everyone laughed when he was offered a chance to milk Daisy and took out a tissue to wrap around her teat. But I never even tried.

I've teased my friend Ann about not getting her ducks in the water, but Ann went to Alaska with her husband and daughter on a long-anticipated vacation—to see *bears*. And up close!

Judy, my best friend from high school, turns out also to be an adventuress. She and her husband and daughter went on safari in Africa. Not the kind where you take in scenic vistas from elegant hotels but the kind where you sleep in tents and are warned not to leave them until dawn because the lions do *not* sleep at night. She could hear them prowling the campsite.

One day tramping in the bush, their little group stood stark still for forty-five minutes as several yards away a male elephant pawed the ground while shaking his ears (not a good sign). Somehow Judy managed ever so carefully to get her camera. Telling this story raises the hair on the back of my neck. She took a picture! And there was another close call: An angry female charged their vehicle when the driver got too close to a herd with a baby elephant to protect. Judy got a picture of that too.

I had a dream recently that I had to deliver a speech to the Explorers Club. I'm not expecting a real invitation to address the Explorers Club in this lifetime. Its members are field scientists and explorers in a variety of arenas, including polar exploration, aeronautics, archaeology, zoology, physics, oceanography, astronomy, ecology, paleontology, mountaineering, and planetology. I struggled to think about what I might tell the

Explorers Club until anxiety woke me up. I think the dream was inspired by a true-life adventure my son Ross had recently written about.

Garry took Ross to Alaska a couple years ago. They lived to tell a tale that Mom wasn't supposed to hear about. Kayaking in frigid waters to see a towering wall of glacier from a "safe distance," they heard an ominous cracking sound to the left. And then another to the right. A chunk of glacier the size of an apartment building broke off and fell into the sea. "What luck!" was a first—but fleeting—thought. The captain back on the ship was thinking he'd just lost all his passengers. He'd never seen such a spectacle in twenty-five years: a fast-moving twenty-foot wave of displaced water was drawing down on a flotilla of tiny kayaks. My husband and son shared one of them. Ross wrote:

> *We both began to paddle as the swell in front of the glacier grew and grew, and a crest began to form. For an absurd moment, our boat did not move. We were paddling in opposite directions. I, trying to about-face and scram, he attempting to square the nose of our bow to the wave. Bugs and Daffy, passing the shotgun barrel back and forth.*
>
> *"Face the wave, Rossy!"*
>
> *By the time the wave was on top of us, the glacier had totally disappeared from view, and the stomach-curdling sight of a frothy crest had formed at the top of the wave. We're going in, I thought.*

All the little boats rose up and over the wave. But behind it was a *bigger* one! Fortunately, everyone survived; they barely got wet. Unfortunately, nobody got pictures. But I see waves everywhere. I can't enjoy rolling hills anymore without imagining those mountainous waves. On a fearlessness scale, I'm about a 1.5.

At some point in my Explorers Club dream, my mother appeared with a copy of a speech I'd left behind. I feel blessed that my parents make cameo appearances in my dreams from time to time. It was just like the old days when she'd pull up at school to deliver the clean gym suit I forgot (every week). Alas, she hadn't brought me a speech for the Explorers Club. It was 4:00 a.m. when I finally woke myself up, but my brain went on churning out ideas for the speech. I went back to sleep when I decided I could talk about the explorers and adventurers I've met on the frontiers of the terra incognita of our reimagined lives.

I was in a hotel room with my daughter when I finally saw my own life reimagined. Rickie turned on the TV—she's a fan of *Today*—and by coincidence that morning my old friends Gene Shalit and Willard Scott were both on the show. I think that's why I saw myself in the picture again too. My Practical Inspiration live-event ideas morphed into a segment for television. Within weeks, I was pitching *Your Life Calling*, about people fifty-plus reinventing their lives, to *Today*'s executive producer, Jim Bell. It was his fortieth birthday. Jim listened as I described stories

I thought would resonate with everyone in his audience and explained that each one would have a reality check. Jim nodded and summed it up: "Aspirational—with a takeaway." He liked the idea. He liked it even better when I found a partner to produce and *pay* for it.

Having collaborated with AARP on an award-winning television special in 2008—*Picking Up the Pieces*, about families of wounded warriors returning from Iraq and Afghanistan—I knew it had a first-rate television production operation. I also knew AARP was eager to reach out to 80 million baby boomers, and no organization knows more about reinvention. The *Today* show, AARP, and me, three trusted American brands, came together to present *Your Life Calling*. But *I* made it happen.

Chapter Twenty-one

Do Something Different

L awrence McRae, of Tuskegee, Alabama, has a gift for making people uncomfortable—but for their own good. At
seventy-five, he should have been in full-swing retirement. He
plays a good game of golf, though a man couldn't get through a
round with him without being asked about his prostate. Lawrence would cross the street to ask a total stranger if he's had his
prostate checked. And frankly, he's seen people cross the street
to avoid him because they knew what was coming. Lawrence
found his calling when he got his own checkup, looked around
the waiting room, and thought, "Gracious, this must be a white
man's disease."

Lawrence was being treated for an enlarged prostate when he
noticed, "Maybe three African-American men were taking the
PSA test [which diagnoses prostate problems, including signs

of prostate cancer], and then you've got ninety-seven white men taking the test." When he learned that African-American men like him are twice as likely to get prostate cancer, that they get it younger, and that they are more likely to die from it, yet very few were getting tested regularly, he thought someone ought to tell them. And it might as well be him.

He printed up homemade brochures, packed a satchel, filled the gas tank, and hit the road. He's been at it for more than a decade with only his Social Security check for funding. His territory sprawls over 250 square miles of the so-called black belt—named for the color of the soil of rural Alabama's poorest communities. He's a man with a mission, spreading the word about the dangers of prostate cancer and the need for testing. He prowls courthouses, visits churches, drops in on barbershops. People call him the Prostate Man. Anywhere men gather, he'll call out, "Let me holler at you." And they'll say, "What?" And he'll reach into the satchel and start talking. He's done it thousands of times. And saved lives.

But Lawrence is up against history. People in the black belt don't trust doctors too much. Not since the infamous Tuskegee syphilis study, conducted between 1932 and 1972. It involved hundreds of black men. According to a report by the Centers for Disease Control, researchers told the men they were being checked for "bad blood," a local term used to describe several ailments, including syphilis, anemia, and fatigue. In truth, most of the men had syphilis, but they were neither told nor treated.

As the CDC report said, "Even after penicillin became the drug of choice for syphilis in 1947, researchers did not offer it to the subjects."

Lawrence showed me around the Tuskegee University Legacy Museum, which documents "forty years of bad blood." President Bill Clinton issued a formal apology to the men who suffered from this sickening study. Today, Tuskegee University is home to the National Center for Bioethics in Research and Health Care and has a cancer research program with a focus on prostate cancer, but people around here have long memories, which makes Lawrence's work all the harder.

But people are learning—sometimes the hard way.

Lawrence to a young man: "You read this book and tell your dad about it, prostate screening. It's got some good information in here. How old is your dad?"

"Fifty-four."

"Yeah, he's not gonna read it. But you read it or let Mama read it, and then tell your dad about it and then make sure Dad goes to the doctor."

"Actually, sir, my dad is going through problems with this now. So we're listening, yes sir."

Lawrence repeats the process day after day, from morning till night. Lying in bed, he'll be planning where to head in the morning.

Along the way, the East Alabama Medical Center has joined him as a partner, but his Social Security check still pays most of the bills. He's still a one-man band banging the drum about prostate awareness. He thinks people listen because he's one of them. He explained to me why an outsider might not have much credibility with local folks. "If you were doing so good somewhere else, why would you come here?" He laughed, but he was serious. "That's how they think."

I got it. You've got to know how people think, if you want to help them think differently.

He never stops. "I went to a golf tournament," he said, "and the guy I was supposed to play with said, 'Look here, don't call my dad and start talking about no prostate. Let's stick to the golf game.'"

Did he? Nah. "I said, 'Make sure your dad gets to the doctor.'"

I play golf—in my way. After seventeen years, I still aspire to a handicap, but I've played with some great golfers. My *Dateline* partner, Stone Phillips, is the most generous golfer I've ever played with, and a round with Bill Murray is the most fun you can have playing golf. I've never played with Matt Lauer, but years ago under the famous awning at 30 Rock, Matt asked about my game, and I said, "Can't hit fairway woods." Later that day a new wood appeared on my desk. It's still my go-to club.

Unfortunately, this chapter's name, "Do Something Different," is a good description of my golf game, because every time I play I do something different. This is not a strategy; I just don't know how to play with consistency. But "Do Something Different" is also a tip the professional golfer Michael Allen got from his wife, Cynthia—and it changed his life.

Maybe you've never heard of Michael Allen. In his early playing days on the PGA tour, he said, laughing, "I was better known as Michael *Who*?" He was also known as the King of Q School. Q School is the grueling annual qualifying process that winnows down thousands of people to the lucky twenty or twenty-five who'll win a PGA tour card. "Qualifying school is probably the most traumatic, difficult tournament that a player will ever play in their life," he said. "It gives you access to your dream, and it takes it away." Nobody has been through it more times than Michael Allen has (eight!). While it says something about his game that he repeatedly had to requalify to keep his tour card, it says far more about his character. He attributes his record to perseverance, resilience, and a stubborn belief in himself.

But belief just wasn't enough with a family to support. Of the two hundred golfers on the PGA tour, Michael figures he ranked about two hundredth. "They used to call me the two-thousand-dollar-a-week man." That was barely breaking even.

Michael finally gave up the dream. Six months later, as assistant pro at the prestigious Winged Foot Golf Club in Mamaroneck, New York, he was hosing the range mats. "That is the ultimate in humility when you're a tour player, and there you are standing in the back maintenance yard of Winged Foot," he admitted. "It wasn't beneath me. I could do it. I was going to support my family." One way or another.

He tried medical sales. He tried building houses. "I was actually able to lose money at that too. I was at such a low we couldn't even buy insurance."

These days, Michael is riding pretty high. I found the story in the sports section of the paper after he accomplished the rare feat of winning PGA Champions tournaments (formerly the Seniors Tour) back to back. Michael is back, and playing better golf in his *fifties* than he ever played before, and beating players he'd never beaten before.

"Here's the story about how I got back," he said. "I am at the Phoenix Open [watching] and a friend says, 'You're better than these guys, why aren't *you* playing?' This friend went to some other guys and put some money together to stake Michael Allen's comeback try and told him, "Go play, you need to be playing."

It's mighty nice having friends like that. But to me the story hinges on Michael's wife Cynthia's support and particularly her advice—which I hope resonates with you as powerfully as it did with me—and with Michael. She said, "If you are going to do this again, you must do *something* different." As Michael explained it to me, she meant, "You can't go about it the same old way. You can't just keep beating your head against the wall, working on the same things. You need a different *approach*."

Michael not only took his wife's advice, he did three things differently.

I'm always amazed that the pros still have teachers, but Michael got a new golf instructor who changed his whole game. "Not just the swing," Michael explained, "but understanding what the clubs do—how important the tools are. What he really changed for me, number one, was passion. As much as I played, I never really had passion like he does."

Michael also changed his approach to fitness. "It's not, 'I'm going to run or be on a bike for an hour.'" He changed the focus to functional fitness. His workouts are designed to enhance his ability to play golf. "Everything I do, every morning when I get up and in the evening when I stretch, has to do with my fitness to be a better golfer."

And he consulted a sports psychologist. "Oh yeah. I've always believed in that. Golf is a little microcosm of life. It's not always what happens to you in life, it's how you deal with what happens. I used to be so caught up in how I did, but now I just enjoy doing it. I have a great time in what I do every day."

Doing something (or a few things) different produced a very different result. Michael was able to repay his friends' investment in a year. He got back on the PGA tour in 2004. A special invitation to play the senior PGA Champions tour in 2009 was a total surprise. "I thought I was past due on some bills or something." Michael surprised everyone by being the winner. "I hit the greatest shot of my life on seventeen, and I was finally winning a tournament," he recalled. "And I was walking to the green, and the camera was right there—one of the first times in my life—and I said, 'It's about friggin' time,' thinking, I've finally gone from Michael Who? to actually winning the senior PGA, and that was an incredible moment for me."

Michael and I were scheduled to talk on a Sunday at the conclusion of a tournament. I arrived to find him way off the leaderboard in the middle of the pack. So I decided to take my bad karma off the course and left to get something to eat. When I returned, Michael had finished the round and was sitting on *top* of the leaderboard—alas, only to lose in a sudden-death playoff. "He hit a perfect shot and I didn't," Michael said with a shrug, adding, "It was a heck of a day. It was a great day."

Michael had earned $1.6 million by the end of the 2012 season. I don't go looking for "success stories" (though you can't help but be happy when nice guys like Michael finish first). The takeaway of the Michael Allen story is Cynthia's perspective on reinvention.

Most of us are not likely to do something *entirely* different. But anyone can do *something* different. And it may be the game-changer. As Michael said, "My perspective on life has changed everything. I am still playing golf, but I have taken a different approach. I know I am trained and ready to do the best I can. I am never going to be Tiger Woods, but I can be pretty darn good."

In his fifties, Michael is a lot better than he was in his thirties. And I'm better in my sixties than I was in my forties, when I started playing golf. Not much better. But I'm always eager to try something different.

Michael shared a tip: "It's better to be *decisive* than right."

Because? "Sometimes we're trying so hard to be right that we're not committed to the shot. You've got to be totally committed. At least you are going to hit a good shot."

In 2000, my friend Roger Rosenblatt wrote a book called *Rules for Aging: A Wry and Witty Guide to Life* (Harcourt). Rule Number 50 is "Change no more than one-eighth of your life at a time." Roger writes, "When you are certain that it is time to become that novelist, sculptor, or watercolorist, change your shoes. See how the new pair fits. Then you might change the side of your head your hair is parted on . . . In a few years, change your glasses."

Thank you, Roger.

Don't overdo it. Just do it a little different.

Chapter Twenty-two

Two Degrees of Cooperation

I remember that deliriously happy first night when Garry and I went to bed with two tiny babies asleep in cribs across the hall. After that my memories get blurrier. Sleep deprivation will do that.

My friend Elena was also the mother of twins old enough that she was advised to let them learn to settle themselves to sleep. The first night two anxious parents waited outside the bedroom door while the wailing went on and on, until a tiny voice from inside the bedroom cried out, "Don't you know there's *babies* in here!"

I've always laughed at that story, but it came to mind when Lauren Walters told me about visiting the pediatric unit of a rural hospital in Rwanda. There were babies in there—hungry and malnourished. The stark images stayed with him, of course, though he never imagined how they would come back into his life.

It's hard to pin down exactly what sixty-one-year-old Lauren Walters does. He's done a lot—lawyer, entrepreneur, NGO consultant, venture capital investor is only a partial list.

"When people ask my wife, 'What does your husband do?' she says, 'I don't know,' and just turns to me," he said. "For a long time people thought I was a spy."

People also call him a connector. And there's no mystery there. Soft-spoken, mild-mannered, and curious, he told me, "I really like people, getting to know them and learning about their lives, finding connections between people or ideas. But I like to let an idea simmer."

Now let me set Lauren on the back burner while I introduce his business partner, Will Hauser, who was twenty-three and on a success track at one of Wall Street's most prestigious firms when he called Lauren for some advice. Lauren has known Will since he was four, and mentored him in college. Will told him, "I want to do something important, something that helps people, and I want to do something entrepreneurial."

He wanted something *more*. Sound familiar?

Lauren Walters and Will Hauser are parallel stories of reinvention—though members of Will's generation are likely to reinvent themselves as many times in their twenties as most of us will in our lives. What we call reinvention is just "the churn" for them.

Penelope Trunk, founder of the Brazen Careerist, says, "Most people have *eight* jobs [my emphasis] before they turn thirty." She adds, "And that's fine. It is nearly impossible to know what career will be a good fit for you until you start trying things." Which I think is true whether you're starting out in life, like Will, or starting anew later in life, like Lauren.

Will's phone call was a "serendipitous moment," Lauren told me, because an idea had been simmering for several years. He had heard Blake Mycoskie, the founder of TOMS Shoes, talk about his "buy a pair, give a pair" concept. And only a few months later, as an adviser to Paul Farmer's Partners in Health, Lauren made that trip to Rwanda.

He said what struck him as he held malnourished babies in his own arms was "I knew that there was a solution." Ready-to-use therapeutic food, a medically formulated paste with micronutrients in a squeezable pouch, was being used throughout Africa, in Latin America, and in many other parts of the world. "But the problem was, there just wasn't enough of it," he said. "Millions of children die every year of starvation, notwithstanding the fact that we know what to do."

When Will called, Lauren connected the dots: the buy-one, give-one concept plus the ready-to-use therapeutic meals. Will was looking for something important that would help people, and Lauren suggested, "Maybe we could do a one-for-one food company. How about that as an idea?" Will thought about it, then told Lauren, "I think it's a great idea."

They decided to start with a snack bar, a very competitive billion-dollar niche in the food industry. The one-for-one concept was that each customer who bought their bar would also be buying a meal for a hungry child somewhere in the world.

"We didn't know anything about the food business," Lauren said. "So it was a matter of pulling in people who did."

A chef was the first person the partners hired. Their "bar guru" was a woman named Bar. "I am not making it up," Lauren said.

He was visiting an old friend. "Well, what are you up to?" she asked. And he said, "I am going to start a food company, a bar company, actually." And she said, "Well, you should talk to my daughter, Bar."

Bar Hogan had been a chef and head of product development at a food and beverage company. While Bar went to work on the product, Lauren and Will kept climbing a steep learning curve: "How do we market? How do we brand? I mean, I had never created a brand for anything, and neither had Will."

"Names are really hard," he told me (as if I hadn't once owned a pair of cats called Boy Kitty and Girl Kitty). Lauren and Will and their mostly millennial brain trust went through hundreds of names. The winner was Two Degrees—a reference to the two degrees of separation between the customer and a hungry child. The next job was designing a logo. They looked at dozens of boring ideas. Finally, Will said, "We should crowd-source it."

It's not true that all great minds think alike, which is the power of intergenerational synergy. Will explained Internet crowd-sourcing to Lauren, and they got eight hundred ideas in three days from all over the world. The winning logo was based on a proposal from a twenty-three-year-old graphic designer in India.

On the front of the package it says, "For every bar you buy, we give a meal to a hungry child." The tagline: "Is good, does good."

"Is good, does good," I observed, "defines what social entrepreneurship really is."

"Exactly," Lauren said. "The core idea behind Two Degrees is to get people to change, to make a choice about their everyday habits." Philanthropy at the checkout counter—a simple idea, though Lauren admitted two and a half years in, "I thought it would be easier than it is."

While Two Degrees Food has already delivered 2.1 million meals in Malawi and Haiti, it has yet to turn a profit. But Lauren is an optimist. He believes, "Anything is possible." He thinks this belief is a legacy of his generational identity, and he aims to pass it on.

"People our age who grew up in the sixties, who cared about what was happening in the world . . . Just because we had families and had to send kids to school and bought cars doesn't mean that we left behind those passions; they just ended up being expressed in different ways. So my expectation is that the young people who have gotten involved with Two Degrees in their teens and early twenties, it's going to stick with them. And whether it becomes the touchstone of what they do, or if they are just receptive to products that have a cause element as opposed to those that don't, I think those things will stick."

And at the end of the day, I believe I found the answer to the question "What does Lauren Walters do?" He's a humanitarian.

The generational divide was a sign of our times. Times have changed. Barbara Chandler Allen, sixty-five, and her son Roger, thirty-one, are partners and cofounders of a nonprofit in Philadelphia called Fresh Artists. "If you look at family businesses across the country, why shouldn't a nonprofit be a family business?" Barbara asked. "The level of trust that exists between a parent and child who want to work together is an extraordinary feeling."

Her partnership with her son is another model of what our two generations could accomplish if we worked together. Barbara's background is in fine art and museums—but that was way back. She was a stay-at-home mom with two sons for twenty years. But she actively sought volunteer roles. And when Roger, her younger son, enrolled in a charter school during high school, she volunteered a lot more. It was a new school with so many needs, and Barbara had the time. "It was exhilarating," she said. "I was learning new things and growing exponentially." A volunteer role evolved into a full-time job in development.

One day, Barbara was driving to an appointment, listening to an interview with Philadelphia's new school superintendent on the radio. It was a call-in show. Barbara was so inspired by what he was saying, she pulled over and called in. She invited him to come see her school. It was a converted office building, but she and Roger had made the halls of this school look like a design museum. The superintendent not only came and saw it, but later returned the invitation. He wanted Barbara to see Philadelphia's new Education Center. He wanted her decorate it. Though Barbara wasn't a designer or decorator or architect, he had called her a "placemaker."

"I sort of sat up and said, 'A *what?*' And he said, 'You make places, you change places.' I didn't know it had a name. I just instinctively would go in and say, 'Well, gee, we could do this, or we could do that.'"

The timing was perfect. Her boys were grown. She was going through a divorce. She'd been fired (twice). She needed a job. This was a big one. The Education Center was a former printing plant in serious need of reinvention. Your old *TV Guide* magazines were probably printed there. It was huge—850,000 square feet. The superintendent wanted to see it filled with children's art.

Barbara remembered being ready to start hanging little pictures everywhere when she realized "they would have looked like flyspecks." But Roger solved the problem in one word: Digital! He said, "The only way to match the artwork with the scale of the building was to blow it up as large as we can." He envisioned taking a high-resolution photograph of a child's little masterpiece and enlarging it through digital printing. Roger, by then, had experience working at a large-format digital shop that made signage for major architectural jobs. Roger said his mom was really good at getting people to donate things. He said to her, "Let's just go ask some printers in town if they would help us."

Barbara enlisted a top architectural photographer to donate his time, and local printers stepped up just as Roger had predicted. The two of them started hanging enormous reproductions of children's art throughout the Education Center, each labeled with the artist's name and grade. The results were astonishing. "Every single time someone would come in and say, 'Can I buy one of those?' And we kept saying no."

Until one day, as they were packing up their tools after hanging an installation, a man stopped to look as he waited for an elevator. He read the wall label explaining the art was the work of a fourth grader. He said, "I don't believe it."

"Well, it is true," Barbara told him. "And I know the child."

The man studied the picture some more. "This isn't what you hear about schools in the news today. What can I do to help?" Barbara and Roger simultaneously realized they were onto something bigger. They went to lunch at a corner hot dog stand and sketched out the concept for Fresh Artists on a paper napkin.

"Everybody tries to figure out how you can possibly get the power of the private sector to bear on the enormity of the problems in public education. How many times in your life have you said, 'What if'? We just stumbled over this solution, Jane."

Paint and paste are smells so evocative of our school days. But these days, the shelves of crayons, pastels, and craft paper we took for granted are empty in many severely underresourced public schools. Barbara said that Philadelphia's allotment per child for art supplies at that time was eighty-three cents a year! Barbara and Roger Allen made children part of the solution.

"This could be in the Metropolitan Museum of Art," Barbara said, as we admired a painting that hangs in Blue Cross headquarters in downtown Philadelphia. Beside it a label says a sixth-grade girl was the artist. Barbara calls her a "child philanthropist." While the child keeps the original, the large-format reproduction is the child's donation. And Blue Cross received the painting as a "thank-you" for making a monetary donation to Fresh Artists. The halls were filled with other "thank-yous." I understood the meaning of "placemaker."

Children's art is transformative in many ways. Barbara described a work of art by another sixth grader. "It was brilliant, extraordinary, strong, powerful, bold." The artist was a boy who'd had some pretty hard knocks in his young life growing up nearby but worlds away from the glamorous downtown office building where his artwork now hangs. She took him to see it. "And he walked closer and closer and he stood in front of it, and then he turned to me and said, 'I guess I really *am* somebody.'"

Donations to Fresh Artists buy art supplies, teacher training, and programs to introduce inner-city kids to careers in the creative arts that they would have no way of knowing about, much less have access to. Both of Barbara's sons have careers in the creative arts. Her older son, Gardner, is an art fabricator who lives in Brooklyn. He illustrated *Pablo, the Philly Philanthropist*, a children's book that tells the story of Fresh Artists. Roger is creative director of Fresh Artists, and Barbara is officially the president.

"I look at where I am now in life," Barbara said. "All of the pieces of what I'm doing with Fresh Artists were there way back forty years ago, when I drove my little red Volkswagen into Philadelphia for the first time, not knowing one soul other than the director of the art museum. I'm still the same person. I'm just older, I'm wiser, I'm even more willing to take risks than I ever was. I've always been pretty bold and pretty fearless. But I think that at sixty-five it's reached almost terrifying proportions.

"We all have threads of things that we've done. I've taken those threads and I've woven them into a new tapestry."

Chapter Twenty-three

Back to School

I acquired a French surname with my marriage, though I don't speak French—or any other language besides English. But I have found the French more hospitable than their reputation, perhaps because my pitiful efforts to communicate provoke sympathy. I walked into a boutique in Paris once and cheerfully called out, "Au revoir!" Immediately sensing my mistake, I began backing out the door just as Garry was stepping in with a hearty "Bonjour!" I *can* say "toilette" well enough to be given directions—in French, which is not so helpful. I think it's probably too late for me to learn a language. But when I noticed French lessons in a box of CDs in a discard pile, I retrieved it and gave it a try in the car as I set out on a road trip. Pretty soon I had to eject the disc because I was getting so involved in the lesson I wasn't concentrating on the road. Was I on the verge of learning a language?

I'll never know. Or will I?

AARP says lifelong learning is a signature trait of my generation. I still have that "I don't remember signing up for this course and haven't studied for the final" nightmare, but far less often than I used to. One of the rewards of aging is that bad dreams spike in the twenties and diminish as we get older.

Maybe learning anxiety does too. By my admittedly small sample of *Your Life Calling* stories, it looks like a lot of us are going back to school—and not just to drop our kids off at college. When Ross was the first of my children to move into a freshman dorm, I was the stereotypical mother *who would not leave*, but it wasn't only because it was so hard to say "Au revoir." I wanted to stay. I yearned for a do-over. I haven't done it yet, but I know a lot of people who have.

Sylvia Abrego-Araiza had a long and often rough road to reinvention. Born to Mexican parents in Texas, Sylvia described her earliest childhood memory riding in the back of a truck as the youngest of three generations of migrant farmworkers. She was working in the fields at the age of four. But her parents were eager for steady work, and they settled down in Idaho. Idaho is not the least ethnically diverse state in the country, but it's far from being the most. And when Sylvia was growing up, it was as white as the inside of an Idaho potato (which is what brought her family to Idaho in the first place). Sylvia went to all-white schools, where as she puts it, she "stuck out like a sore thumb."

She still recalls with glistening eyes the day she found out where she stood. "The girls—maybe ten or twelve of us—would go out there and play as a group and have a great time," Sylvia told me. Sylvia recalled always trying to fit in until the day she was pointedly left out. "I remember this girl taking me behind the door, and she said, 'You are not gonna play with us anymore. We don't want you playing with us.' And she went on to call me a lot of names, very, very derogatory words. And I was so hurt, and I was just standing there behind the door, and I'll never forget that."

How does a little girl respond to such a brutal rejection? "I did not stoop to her level," Sylvia said quietly. "I didn't call her names. I went outside and just stood there. I could see them playing without me. And then I saw the boys playing, and I went over to them and watched them. And one boy who was riding a skateboard asked me if I wanted to learn to ride. I said sure. I started playing with the boys."

Sylvia's resilience did not fully compensate; she was always made to feel like an outsider. Yet out of the pain she found the determination to excel. Her high school yearbook tells a story of not merely fitting in but standing out—Cinco de Mayo queen, a class officer, and an honor student heading for college. But young dreams were derailed by some bad choices—including two failed marriages. She was a small child when her family left the Rio Grande Valley, but decades later that's where she went to start over. She married again, rediscovered her faith, got a job, and just before Christmas got laid off.

"I was working as a quality assurance monitor for an employment agency, and there was a reorganization," Sylvia said. "I was devastated. I did not know which way I was going to turn. I had a new husband, a new home, a new car, new furniture, and no job."

But for a long time, even before she was laid off, Sylvia's son had been prodding her to go back to school. "I had put school on the back burner for so long, it wasn't even a thought, and I was happily employed, so I hadn't even considered it," she explained. "And when I found myself without a job, the first thing I thought of was 'I need to get a *job*!' I was frantically just looking for a job.

"And then I heard this little voice inside of me, and I do believe the voice inside of me was God speaking to me. I just heard Him say, 'You need to go back to school.' And I was like, *'What?'* And He was like, 'You need to go back to school—finish what you started.'"

Sylvia prayed about it and talked it over with her husband. She told him she knew their financial situation wasn't that strong, but God was telling her to do this, and she thought she should. He was fully supportive. So in January 2004, at age forty-four, Sylvia enrolled at South Texas College. She studied for a degree in applied science for social work, but learned so much more.

"I was taking drug and alcohol courses, and it was like therapy for me. I was starting to unravel some things in my life, things that I had kept inside for so long, suppressed feelings, issues that I hadn't dealt with that were unresolved. There was a part of me that needed to heal, needed to bring these issues out in the open. There were a lot of tears in that class," she said with some fresh tears, then smiling, added, "But I did get an A." And she found a calling. When she started to heal herself, she realized that she needed to help others.

Sylvia graduated with a job waiting for her. Hidalgo County, at the southern tip of Texas, was very much in need of her skills as a substance abuse counselor. She specializes in teens who've made some bad choices—a page out of her own life story. Sylvia told me, "I aim to reach them with love, understanding, and compassion. Inside each and every one of us is that potential, that ability, that gift that needs to be unwrapped and developed."

She has chosen a profession that can be full of disappointment. Things don't always work out for the young people in her charge. I asked her how she defined success in light of harsh reality. She responded, "I would define success as pouring yourself into what you do, into what you have a passion for doing, giving compassion to others, and basically changing the world one individual at a time."

The idea that it *is* possible to learn something new in midlife can be exhilarating. Older learners come equipped with toolboxes of knowledge and experience waiting to be applied in new ways. Remember how Tripp Hanson learned anatomy by choreographing it like a musical number and practicing it the same way he'd learned dance combinations onstage? I love the way Tripp puts things. He says, "The grace of going to school later in your life is that you know what you need."

In recent years research has debunked the old notion that we lose brain cells as we age. Neuroscientists have been surprised at the brain's plasticity. As long as you keep stretching your capacity to learn, the brain keeps building neural connections. Neuroscientists also say that stretching is precisely what keeps the aging brain agile. Barbara Strauch, the *New York Times* health editor and author of *The Secret Life of the Grown-Up Brain*, writes with great flourish about the flexibility that occurs, surprisingly, when people are in their fifties and sixties. She includes an intriguing interview with Dr. Kathleen Taylor, a professor at Saint Mary's College in California and an expert on adult learning. Dr. Taylor speaks of "jiggling your synapses" by getting out of your comfort zone to learn new things. "As adults we have these well-trodden paths in our synapses," she says. "We have to crack the cognitive egg and scramble it up. And if you learn something this way, when you think of it again you'll have an overlay of complexity you didn't have before—and help your brain keep developing as well."

Colleges and universities are cultivating older learners. Mary Reed was able to earn a master's degree without having an undergraduate diploma. Antioch's Institute of Open Education awarded her credits for life and work experience. Her class was filled with adults in their thirties and forties.

Chocolatier Antoinette Little is thinking about going for a college degree. She's an experienced learner after dozens of culinary classes. Her anxiety about being older by thirty years than the other students in culinary school dissolved as quickly as confectioners' sugar in a pastry mix when she recognized the secret advantage of her age. Not only did the younger students look up to her but she was far more likely to have done the homework.

A generation ago, working your way through college as alpaca farmer Thomas Betts did was common. Catherine Zimmerman worked her way through college in her *fifties*, and with a full-time job and three children.

I met Catherine as we scouted an outdoor location for a shoot. She is an award-winning documentary filmmaker, but it became obvious there was more than met the eye when she started critiquing the backyard landscaping. Thirty years ago, Catherine was one of the pioneers who proved that you didn't need to be a man to be a cameraman. She was among the pretty, long-haired girls turning up in newsrooms around the country back in the seventies—the ones who aspired to be behind the camera or, more literally, underneath it. "They gave me the biggest (and heaviest) camera," she said, "because I was low on the totem pole." She is still toting a heavy camera and the gear that goes with it. But she can't do that forever.

A single mother of three, Catherine was an empty nester with no nest egg. Retirement wasn't even an option. For her it wasn't a yearning for something different but a necessity.

Catherine started looking for something she could do "for the next thirty years" about ten years ago. It wasn't surprising that her first thought was gardening. She grew up on a farm in Ohio and in her suburban Washington neighborhood had earned a reputation as the "lawn queen." But she recognized that being good at gardening didn't mean people would pay her to do it. (I like to think I'm a better than average singer, but nobody would buy a ticket to hear me.) To make a living as a landscape gardener, Catherine realized she needed credentials. She found a program, offered by the U.S. Department of Agriculture, in horticulture and landscaping design. She was shaking when she took her first test, but like Sylvia, she got an A. For three years she juggled motherhood, her job, and school. "It meant that all my evenings were tied up with doing homework, basically," she said. "I had to turn down some paying work to make it happen." And a funny thing happened along the way: "I always thought I was so darn good at gardening. Then I learned how darn bad I was."

Her grass was green, the flowers were lovely, but she noticed the fireflies were gone. "I'd be lucky if I saw maybe five fireflies in one night," she said. "I made the connection that it was *me*. I did that!" The lawn queen, she said with disdain, was a "reckless gardener," addicted to pesticides.

She started thinking differently about her lawn and garden—looking into organics and wanting to know more about native plants. The Department of Agriculture didn't have a course in native plants, but they suggested that perhaps she could *teach* one.

Like Jenny Bowen, Catherine already excelled at research. She went in search of experts—and learning from them has become one herself. Her particular passion and expertise is meadow making. She has self-published a beautiful book, *Urban and Suburban Meadows: Bringing Meadowscaping to Big and Small Spaces.* Her dining room is the packing and distribution center. She mails the copies herself.

Catherine has made a big investment in her future, and the payoff remains in the future. She still uses her camera to pay the bills. But as the saying goes, "Gardeners are people who believe in the future." And when I asked Catherine if she felt worried about the uncertainty of her future, she said, "I'm not frightened by it . . . I think it's because I draw something from somewhere, maybe from the soil. But it's there and I feel grounded."

Chapter Twenty-four

The Call of the Wild

W e're all singing that same song," Barbara O'Grady told me. Barbara's song has an almost primal undertone, a call of the wild. Sometimes she has bears in her yard. Or bison or deer—which can be really dangerous (as her little poodle learned the hard way) if they have fawns. Barbara lives alone with her poodle, working as a part-time certified interpretive guide at Yellowstone National Park. Her job is telling visitors the story of the park. Her own story is about as compelling.

In 2006, Barbara was a married, working mother of four in suburban Denver, as she put it, "living other people's definition of who I was, and it was uncomfortable. It was unfulfilling in many ways. I felt inadequate. I felt like I couldn't do anything the way I wanted to do it because I didn't have the time. There wasn't enough of me to go around. A lot of the time I felt like not the best mother, not the best worker. And there was something very important missing from my life."

Barbara grew up in Connecticut and had never been west of the Hudson River until the summer after her freshman year at Vassar. She signed up for a six-week field trip led by her freshman geology professor. They drove all the way to Seattle, visiting national parks along the way. She calls it a life-changing experience. Heading back east at the end of the summer, she vowed to live in the West one day. That fall she declared a major in geology.

But as in geological time, change for Barbara evolved slowly. Although she did move west, it wasn't quite the life she had imagined.

As a young wife, Barbara followed her husband to Houston when he got a job in the oil industry. With her master's in geology, Barbara had her pick of job offers in the oil industry too. But when children arrived—four of them, including a set of twins—she put her career on hold for eleven years to be a stay-at-home mother. The family moved to Denver. Her decision to go back to work was inspired by her reluctance to return to Houston, where her husband had a new job opportunity.

"For the first time in my marriage," she told me, "I said, 'I'm not going.' And he said, 'Well, if you want to stay in Denver, then you're going to have to get a job.'"

For the next seventeen years she worked for the Colorado

Department of Public Health and Environment. Is there any state in the country more evocative of natural beauty than Colorado, with its soaring Rocky Mountains? Where would a geologist be happier? But Barbara was not happy. Her job was protecting the environment, but her view of it? She worked in a windowless office. It was suffocating on many levels.

She yearned for open spaces. When her children were old enough that she didn't have to be home all the time, she took her first solo road trip.

"Where'd you go, what did you do?" I asked her, sensing a big first step in her reinvention.

"I went to Glacier National Park to take a class on wolves."

"Wolves?"

Barbara laughed. Her children had been surprised too. They said, "What's going on with Mom?" But something was calling to her. She explained, "You know, part of my consideration for my children was how do I want them to perceive me? Do I want them to perceive me as a suburban housewife that's unhappy and not willing to step out of her comfort zone to go after what I really wanted, or do I want them to think of me as someone who is courageous and brave and intelligent and competent and willing to take risks and be adventurous?"

Her children, then in high school, were becoming more independent. She was in her forties, that decade now recognized as the "trough" of dissatisfaction. "It was something very, very strong inside of me. I knew that there was more out there and I needed to find it, and I didn't have that much time to do it."

Barbara was also recovering from her first serious illness, an autoimmune disorder called idiopathic urticaria. "Urticaria" means hives, which can come in some pernicious and debilitating forms. And "idiopathic" means no known cause. I needed no translation because, as I'll explain later, I knew about idiopathic urticaria from personal experience. Barbara wondered if she'd ever get better, but she did.

"It had a lot to do with my going to Glacier. I had that feeling I'd better take advantage of feeling good. It could come back." On her way home, she happened to see a newspaper in a diner, and a headline caught her eye. She remembers it was something like "Democrats are an endangered species in Wyoming." And she was inspired. "I thought, 'Oh my gosh, I can't let them be an endangered species in Colorado.' I must declare my candidacy."

She actually ran for the Colorado State Senate in 1998 but lost. "I wouldn't be here if I had been elected." In the end, politics wasn't her calling.

But in subsequent years, she found many ways to declare her independence. There were more solo vacations, including a group canoe expedition to the most remote place in the lower forty-eight states, though she'd never paddled a canoe before.

Back in her windowless office, Barbara kept a live streaming video of Old Faithful open on the computer screen on her desk. Every morning, she logged on to her computer to see what was doing in Yellowstone. But, "it came to a point where that didn't do it for me anymore. I actually had to be there."

She scanned the Yellowstone website looking for volunteer opportunities, just to stay connected to the park. For example, park rangers take a lot of notes, and Barbara offered to transcribe those notes in her spare time.

On a tour of the Yellowstone archive, she asked, "Would you ever have any need for a volunteer?" When the archivist found out she was a geologist, she suggested Barbara send her information—which she did the moment she returned home. Within twenty-four hours, she had a response. Yellowstone had a program of volunteer professionals. Would Barbara be interested in doing a paleontology project for them? They required a commitment of at least a month—or more. For Barbara, this was that door swinging on a hinge moving inexorably into her future.

"I said yes right away. I thought, 'Oh, my God, this is it. This is it! Nothing's going to stop me. This is my time.'" She was fifty-five. "I didn't want to wait until I was sixty-five to do what I really wanted." She made a spreadsheet to figure out how to retire that year.

As she described the moment to me, I anticipated what was coming—a decisive *dividing line* between her past and her future. "Your children were already living independent lives, but your marriage wasn't going to survive this," I ventured.

She nodded. "I think my husband and I both knew it at the

time—that this was a real pivotal point. And I think we were realizing that our visions of the future were very, very different." Barbara was almost crying now. "It was a very hard price to pay."

She took that volunteer job. A month later she'd signed her retirement papers and was pulling out of her Denver driveway in a car packed with household items—alone.

"Was it an experiment?" I asked.

"No, no, no," she said. "There was no turning back at that point."

Her only regret is the pain she left behind. She says that her former husband jokes ruefully that he must be the only man who ever lost his wife to a national park. For Barbara, it was truly a love affair with Yellowstone.

She's started a business, Wild Bear Adventures. Her website beckons: "When was the last time you heard a wild wolf howl? Filled your lungs with the sweet scent of sage? Watched a bison calf kick up its heels? Felt the first rays of morning sun warm you? Been a while?" She leads guided tours of Yellowstone.

Standing with Barbara in her new habitat, looking out on the breathtaking vista, I ask if one could really see wild bears.

"Hopefully, you see wild bears," she replied. "We might even see some wild bears later on today, which would be really great." I confess I wasn't terribly disappointed when we didn't. But the bison herd I did see was spectacular, and I felt lucky to see a newborn—from a comfortable distance with binoculars.

Barbara always carries binoculars. You never know what you might see in Yellowstone. But she found what she was looking for. "I'm not searching anymore, I have arrived. I'm here. This is it, this is life, this is me. Yellowstone for me is the answer to the question 'Why?'"

Chapter Twenty-five

Reality Checks

Vacationing in Tuscany over the years, Bill and Patty Sutherland, of Dallas, Texas, fell in love with the vineyards, the olive groves, the gently rolling hills, and the food. "We had too much wine at lunch one day," Patty said, "and the rest is history."

Bill was fifty-four and Patty fifty-three when they saw Podere Poggio Castagni, a three-hundred-year-old stone farmhouse perched on a hilltop, surrounded by vineyards and olive trees. "It was totally dilapidated," Patty said, but they could see possibilities—even though it was a foggy day, and they didn't discover the "disaster" inside until later. But they could tell it was their dream home, with a view from atop the Tuscan Hills, and they pictured themselves living there.

"I wanted to be able to make my own wine and make my own olive oil and have a garden," Bill said. "That was heaven for me."

"Good thing you didn't marry me," I teased him, knowing he had found the perfect partner in Patty.

Bill and Patty had been sweethearts in high school who went different ways and married different people. Patty had been widowed young and had raised two sons, working as an artist and graphic designer. Bill was divorced when their paths crossed a second time, and they fell in love all over again. They often vacationed in Tuscany and knew the area pretty well.

Two years after they bought their dream house, and spent vacations fixing it up, they made the decision to go "all in." They sold their house in Dallas and Bill's real estate business, as well as the gourmet shop he had on the side, and made a permanent move to Tuscany. When people found out what they were doing, they often asked, "What are you running away from?" Patty said something I'd heard before. "We weren't running away from anything. We were running toward something. We wanted a new adventure."

Bill says he's the romantic. Patty calls herself the realist, as she listed all the reasons why uprooting their lives and living abroad made perfect sense. "We both were married very young, we had kids very young, and we just never had the adventure. We wanted to get out of our comfort zone. And anyway," she added, "what's the worst thing that could happen? I think if you stay a little scared that's a good thing. You know you're alive."

But Bill was practical enough to know that if they were going to live in Tuscany on a permanent basis, they had to come up with a business concept. He was drawn to the idea of doing something with food. And food is a big part of the attraction of Tuscany. But *home-cooked* Tuscan dinners were the Sutherlands' revelation—four-hour affairs with plate after plate of appetizers, three or four pastas, numerous meat courses, and a full array of desserts. The best cooks in Tuscany, Bill concluded, were the grandmothers—not professional chefs. That was the inspiration for their cooking school.

Tuscan Women Cook is in session five months a year. People come in small groups from all over to learn traditional Tuscan culinary traditions—"poor food," which, Bill explained to me, was created in times gone by, by people who couldn't afford to have chickens year-round, which meant they didn't have eggs all the time. And so they made a pasta called "*pici.*" It's simply flour and water—and it's incredible.

Bill set me up with a grandmother (who looked younger than I do) to teach me how it's done. It took me back. Where I come from, we didn't call it "pasta," but Mom's noodles made from scratch were my favorite birthday dinner. My kids' favorite birthday dinners were dining out, but one day I saw a recipe for "Hoosier Noodles" in a magazine—flour, water, eggs, pinch of salt—and it sounded familiar, and easy enough. Hundreds of times, I'd watched my mother work the dough and spread it flat with a rolling pin until it covered the kitchen table in an irregular shape—like an amoeba, now that I think about it. I remembered her technique of hanging doughy ribbons on a broomstick propped between kitchen chairs to dry. My children had noodles made from scratch for dinner that night. According to the magazine, authentic Hoosier Noodles are served on a bed of mashed potatoes, but I served them plain, like my mother did. They were tough as shoelaces but the flavor was just right.

I'm not really as helpless in the kitchen as I make out, and while I suspect the same of Patty (she's an artist, but not in the kitchen), I was amazed that she was game to start a cooking school. "I guess I felt comfortable with it because there would be a lot of coordinating to take care of," she told me. "I wouldn't have to be on the front line with the skillets."

Bill is the gourmet chef. He runs the cooking part. But after morning classes, followed by a spectacular luncheon, school adjourns and Patty leads rambling tours of the village, exploring its culture, history, and art.

Year by year, the business took hold. It was a labor of love, but make no mistake, it was hard work launching a business in a foreign country rather famous for an impenetrable bureaucracy and speaking what the Sutherlands describe as "tourist Italian." And there were times when Patty—but never Bill—was tempted to pack it in.

"That happens to a lot of expats," she said, "usually after about two years, when the honeymoon is over and you realize that the culture is not going to adapt to you. We're very isolated in the winter up here on this hill. We had grandchildren who were growing up. We were missing a lot of the holidays." So she surprised Bill with a condo in Dallas. That was the compromise—six months in Tuscany and six months in Texas—with regular maintenance visits in between.

Bill's health kept him on a tether. Right after they'd made a bid on their Tuscan dream house, he had gone into the hospital for heart surgery. He was in the recovery room when Patty gave him the good news: "We got the house!" For some people, a heart condition might have been a reason to stay put and live minutes away from the best cardiology hospital in the country, which happens to be in Dallas. For Bill, it was another reason to go for the adventure. "I don't want to have regrets in life," he said.

About eight years ago, Patty stayed in Tuscany to mind the school while Bill went home to see a doctor about something new. "I thought it was some sort of gastro problem or something," he said. "When I got there, they start using the big C word. It's a type of lymphoma that is curable to an extent, but it's one that can always come back." After he went through chemo, "and all that stuff," as he put it, Bill returned to Tuscany.

"The good news," he told me, "is that two weeks ago I did a PET scan and I'm one hundred percent clear. The bad news is I have congestive heart failure."

In fact, while we talked in the courtyard of Podere Poggio Castagni—a setting worthy of *Architectural Digest*—Bill was hooked up to a portable IV. And a physician—his brother-in-law—was standing nearby. He'd made the trip especially to enable Bill to do the interview. It was that serious.

Because of Bill's cancer, a heart transplant wasn't an option. He was hooked up to the kind of device former Vice President Dick Cheney had worn before his heart transplant. "They put a pacemaker in me and put a defibrillator in me. There's not a new Mercedes on the road that's got better equipment than I have installed in me," Bill boasted. When I packed to leave Tuscany, I was pretty sure the Sutherlands would be leaving soon, too.

Patty sounded philosophical. "Whatever happens we don't want to say, 'I wish we would have done that.' I want my grandchildren and great-grandchildren to look at the photo albums and say, 'That was my crazy grandmother and she really had an adventure.'"

I'm not an adventurer, but I haven't had many regrets. I can say now and without apology, I have been extraordinarily lucky. As I've heard Al Franken, a comedian who reinvented himself as a United States senator, say, "Growing up almost anywhere in suburban America in the fifties was to feel lucky." We took our possibilities for granted. We really believed those Red Ball Jets could make us run faster. That Cheerios gave us Go Power. We truly did have the best schools in the world. And in those days a middle-class family could send two daughters to college on one paycheck, with no loans.

Our kids are growing up with a more tenuous hold on their dreams. And not all of us will catch the wave of possibility that I'm suggesting we prepare for. I'm a believer in the future, but

I'm no Pollyanna. Like Patty Sutherland said, "I always hope for the best, but plan for the worst." And like Patty, I self-identify as neither an optimist nor a pessimist but a realist.

I try to choose stories that are inspirational and aspirational, but they all come with reality checks—like Trudy Lundgren's story of life in the Catbird Seat. You'll recall that when the engine blew, it cost $20,000 to replace it. And while Trudy is not as disposed as I am to ask "what if?," one of my questions to her was, "What if you get sick?"

In March 2011, about a year after our interview, Trudy noticed a lump in her breast and was diagnosed with cancer. Through two surgeries and radiation treatments, Trudy never lost her sense of humor, blogging to her friends and new fans, "Good thing I can still drink beer!"

She stayed positive and hopeful, and after months of treatments, Trudy became cancer-free and remains so today. And she and Lisa are back on the road, but with a new mission—raising money for cancer research and treatment. In 2012 and 2013 she walked in marathons for Avon Walk for Breast Cancer in Houston, Texas, raising money for the charity. "I'm living my life. I'm not waiting around to get old." That's what Trudy told me before, and it's still her mantra.

I did not foresee Anthony Tata's reality check. He went from brigadier general to Raleigh, North Carolina, superintendent of schools. But after eighteen months, he was fired. I guess his leadership style didn't mesh so well with the school board. But he landed on his feet. Today Tony heads up the North Carolina Department of Transportation.

When reality meets reinvention, reality doesn't *always* win. To my happy surprise, I found out that the Sutherlands are still in Tuscany after all. Bill's heart condition has improved, but they've made some concessions to reality. They sold their lovingly renovated Tuscan villa and downsized to an apartment in the village. Still, the cooking classes are fully booked.

My friends have been a thread through this book. They call. They write. They take me to dinner and a show. Plenty of research says social connections are a better predictor of longevity and happiness than almost anything else. So if I live another thirty or forty years I have many friends to thank. Like Belinda who surprised herself by remarrying after twelve years at the age of fifty-eight. A mark of Jeffrey's devotion to her was moving back from London after a twenty-year career there. But not before her friends Jane and Katy dropped into the London flat to share a bit of their honeymoon!

And what became of my friend Meg ("What am I going to do for forty years?"). It's an amazing story, actually. She said, "When I stop and think about it I even amaze myself!" She doesn't have much time to stop and think about it.

At fifty-four, as she put it, she was "third founder of a tech start-up" with two of her adult children (whom I've known since nursery school!). Five years later Paperless Post has sixty employees, has sent 85 million custom digital cards, and is moving to a 12,500-square-foot office. "After a twenty-three-year leave of absence to raise those children, I am again using my law degree (and every cell in my brain) ten hours a day as the CAO of a dynamic growing company."

She says to me now, "Your faith that I would have another chapter was very meaningful to me. I thought I was fooling you or you were being kind, but it happened."

I always believed in Meg's passion—I just didn't foresee where it would lead. I don't think Meg will have time to teach me how to cook anytime soon. Frankly, cooking was the passion I thought she'd follow, which is a cautionary tale about how the people closest to us may suffer from lack of imagination. It's not always good advice to just "follow your passion." There may be something more.

Chapter Twenty-six

Talk Therapy

Several years ago, reading an article about Meredith Vieira's arrival as host of *Today*, I stumbled upon this line near the end: "Morning hosts are supposed to seem normal. That's the quality that got Jane Pauley her job on *Today*." Mystery solved at last!

I used to be famously "normal." One president of NBC News said, "Jane Pauley has the best mental health in the business." At the time, I probably agreed. In any event, I was probably about as "normal" as I appeared to be.

It's said that a quarter of families are touched by a psychiatric disorder. For the first fifty years of my life, my family was not among them. Family history? We had none, at least none that I, or anyone living, knew about.

But family history and family secrets can sometimes be the

same thing. Twelve years ago, I was diagnosed with bipolar disorder. It came out of the blue, on the heels of a year and a half of a pernicious form of hives—idiopathic urticaria edema. *Urticaria*, as you may remember from Barbara O'Grady's story, means hives. *Idiopathic* means cause unknown. *Edema* means swelling. In my case it most often occurred in the soft tissue of my eyes or lips, which was awkward given that I had a career on television. But after swelling began to appear in my throat—which can be fatal—there were five months of aggressive medication followed by another five months of antidepressants to treat a common side effect of the medication. It was a kind of one-two punch. When the symptoms of hypomania were recognized, the best medical guess was that I had had a previously unrecognized genetic vulnerability to bipolar disorder, and that the combination of medications was a contributing factor in revealing it.

After twelve years, I've not had a second episode. I try to do everything that's within my power to prevent a recurrence. I am fortunate to be productive again, but I am aware of my limits. I can't avoid stress entirely, but I avoid it when I can. I take meds every day—no holidays. I monitor my moods: Am I talking too loud or too fast? Am I sleeping too much or too little? Neuroscientists have told me that disregulated sleep is known to be a factor—a symptom, a trigger, or both—in many major brain disorders. I've become a sleep evangelist.

A generation ago, people didn't talk about cancer. Today we wear pink ribbons and run "for the cure." Now people are starting to talk more openly about psychiatric disorders. I think in part it's because new words in our everyday vocabulary have begun to change the way we think about and understand the brain. For example, I often describe getting things "on my hard drive," and you know what I mean, though honestly, how many of us really have a good grasp of what a hard drive is? But tech savvy or not, we use this new terminology when we talk about the brain.

For example, I overheard this conversation at my dining room table. My friend Judy was telling Garry about her golf lessons with an instructor named Lou. One exercise involved a repetitive swing, repeating, "Take it to Lou, take it to Lou."

I heard Garry say, "You were rewiring your brain."

Then Judy said, "Exactly."

Our parents never had that thought. We take it for granted. We think about the brain differently.

By happenstance, I was diagnosed with bipolar disorder on the first day of a six-week sabbatical from NBC. It had been my intention to work on a memoir with a working title that suddenly took on new meaning: *Skywriting: A Life Out of the Blue.* Six weeks became six months. I recovered and returned to work in September 2001. The tenth of September to be precise. The next day was September 11. That put everything in a new perspective. I didn't return to my memoir for another couple of years.

After my book came out ten years ago, my first invitation to give a talk came from Robert Desimone, Ph.D., the director of the McGovern Institute for Brain Research at MIT. I was subsequently invited to join a leadership advisory board at the McGovern. As you may imagine, this is one of the brightest spots on my résumé.

I'm pretty well recovered from the impostor syndrome, in part because I'm not that famous anymore. I blend. I'd just finished shooting the Jan Erickson story in Boulder and was having something to eat outdoors at the patio restaurant of a fine Denver hotel. It was a balmy Saturday evening. A young crowd was beginning to gather—you could feel the party vibes. I was a party of one, and nobody paid me the slightest notice until a homeless man ambled by, did a double take, and asked for my autograph. I obliged. He returned a few minutes later and asked for some money. Again, I obliged. Noticing hotel security moving our way, he broke off an increasingly animated discussion of Katie Couric's new show and his ideas about renewable energy and melted into the evening. The majority of homeless men and women are suffering from a psychiatric disorder or addiction.

I'm accustomed to encounters with strangers. A lady followed me out of the hair salon. She said she needed some advice. Should she cut her hair or leave it long? She couldn't decide.

Pretty soon she got to the problem I'd been expecting. She said she couldn't seem to make decisions anymore and was driving her husband crazy. She said, "I think I might have what *you* have." She was thinking about bipolar disorder.

Personally, a celebrity is the last person I'd consult about medical matters, but I'm always happy to talk. Sometimes people tell me I'm the first person they've ever talked to. Once in my gynecologist's waiting room a woman took me aside to thank me. She explained that she and her teenage children had seen me on TV talking about bipolar disorder. She said her ex-husband struggled with bipolar disorder too. And after the interview she and her kids talked about it—for the first time!

When I was a teenager, my mother had ovarian cancer. Fortunately, she survived, but we *never* talked about it. I can only wonder now what else we weren't talking about. Talking is pretty important. That's the role I play in mental health advocacy. I call it talk therapy.

Talking about bipolar disorder was the easiest decision I ever made. And I've had no reason to regret it. It's even possible that talking about it has helped keep me well. There's abundant research that giving support is as therapeutic as getting it. Sometimes a hopeful mother will tell me that her child is "doing so well, we're looking forward to getting off the meds." I will take her hands in mine and say, "The goal is not to get off the meds; the goal is to do everything possible to prevent another episode." I can't say having bipolar disorder has been a blessing, but having an advocacy role has been. I'm tempted to say it's even given more purpose to my life, but I'd have to credit a woman named Joan for the idea.

I was the keynoter at an event where therapists and clinicians who worked with indigent people with mental health disorders and addictions were getting some well-deserved acknowledgment. Joan was one of the award winners. She clearly hadn't expected it and nervously approached the podium and stood awkwardly at the microphone. Fumbling for words, she finally said: "Well, I guess I'd just like to thank the clients for giving *purpose* to my life." The room went silent. Nothing in the prepared remarks on my lap was nearly as inspiring. In the pressure of the moment, I wondered if Joan had even heard herself say what the rest of us found so inspiring, so I repeated it for her. A job like hers must be very demanding. But at the end of the day, to recognize that the clients—whether struggling successfully or just struggling—give her life *purpose* is to be blessed with a new perspective on her work. And that's a kind of reinvention.

Meanwhile, I've had to reinvent my personal narrative. I was pretty invested in that reputation for being "normal." I probably helped cultivate it, but I enjoy telling a story I heard told by a Nobel laureate. He said that the daughter of Sigmund Freud's best friend was training to be a psychoanalyst and accordingly was required to undergo analysis. She dearly hoped that Freud would do it, but because of their personal relationship he was reluctant. Finally, he relented. And later, when the analysis was complete, he is said to have told her, "I always liked you, but now that I know you have problems, I like you even better."

Chapter Twenty-seven

Just Say Yes

People often ask me, "Who's been your favorite interview?" I've interviewed thousands of people. But the answer is easy. Michael J. Fox. We're not close personal friends, but we go way back. It would be hard to talk about my personal reinvention story without telling the story about how he had called NBC ten years ago, volunteering to be my final *Dateline* interview. When *Dateline* celebrated its twentieth anniversary in 2012, I was invited to reprise our interview and had a chance to ask him why. He said, "You'd been there at so many important times in my life; I wanted to be there for one of yours."

I first interviewed Michael when you would have known him better as Alex P. Keaton—if you'd known of him yet. He appeared on *Today* to promote a new NBC sitcom called *Family Ties*, and he was not supposed to be the "star." He was just a young Canadian actor trying to make it in Hollywood. But overnight, he became a big star! I interviewed him regularly over the years as his star ascended. *Back to the Future* propelled him into superstardom. I happened to be on the set with him during the filming of *Doc Hollywood* in Florida where he first recognized a symptom that would later be diagnosed as Parkinson's disease. It was a troubling tremor in his pinkie finger. He didn't tell me, of course.

I explained in my memoir that as *Dateline* prepared a one-hour special edition, "Jane Pauley Signs Off," in 2003, only a few people at NBC knew about my illness. I hadn't written *Skywriting* yet. But my own illness wasn't far from my thoughts as we talked about how Michael hadn't made much accommodation for his. Despite Parkinson's, I noted that in only the previous year, he had written a book, created a TV pilot, made a movie, testified before Congress, and raised millions of dollars for Parkinson's research. And he and his wife, Tracy Pollan, had a fourth child!

"If it was me," I'd said (thinking about my own illness), "I'd be relaxing, taking it easy, conserving my energy . . ." And Michael replied, "What would you be conserving your energy *for?*" In classic *Dateline* vernacular: "It changed my life forever." I decided then and there to say yes to the daytime show.

I don't recall it as a conscious recalibration of my diagnosis and my life. But underlying that "yes" was a fundamental determination to keep on *living* with it. Michael inspired that.

There's a lot of that going around. I think of Bill Sutherland, who has managed to make a remarkable life, despite a heart condition. And Antoinette Little, who reinvented herself because of a diagnosis.

Dawn Nakamura Kessler has lived on the knife's edge since undergoing open-heart surgery—twice—in her twenties. She was a very sick young woman, with bacterial endocarditis, an inflammation of the lining of the heart, but was also a stunning beauty. And a heart surgeon lost his heart to her.

But Dawn's happily-ever-after was clouded by the reality she saw every single day—the big scar down the front of her chest. She had no expectation of living a long life. She had one goal—to live long enough to see her handsome son graduate from high school. And she did.

After she had reached that goal, she was looking for a new one. She heard about a contest: A beauty products company was looking for "real life" models. And, if you'll pardon the expression, Dawn is still drop-dead gorgeous. What did she have to lose? She entered the contest. While she did not win, being a finalist inspired her to go for it and, at the age of forty-nine, try a career in modeling.

Dawn's first professional go-see for a job was a big reality check. The other girls were teenagers. "They looked like girls my son would date," Dawn said. She was tempted to flee to the parking lot and drive home, but she didn't and she *did* get the job. And continues to get jobs. More and more, advertisers are seeking a grown-up look, having noticed that we older consumers are still a viable market. It's getting harder to ignore us. Baby boomers account for $2 trillion in consumer spending a year, which is about 70 percent of America's wealth. Dare we call her lucky? Yes! Dawn's timing was perfect. And she embraces her future with optimism. As she put it, "I don't think I've had all my 'wonderfuls' yet."

I've had more than my share of "wonderfuls." The daytime show was a wonderful opportunity, but a bigger challenge than I expected—though I went into it knowing the odds of success were long. I'd be opposite Dr. Phil everywhere I wasn't against Oprah. I prepared the kids accordingly, telling them my definition of success was having the courage to say yes. Which brings me back to Michael J. Fox. He's a big believer in yes. In our most recent interview in 2012, he explained, "No doesn't move you forward. Say yes more than no."

Michael is a personal inspiration to so many people. Like Orlando Ward, he's in the "hope business." Do you remember what Michael called his memoir? *Lucky Man.* He tells a story about waiting for an elevator in a mirrored vestibule, just as his meds were starting to wear off. Catching a glimpse of a bent and shaking old man, he realized he was looking at his own reflection. What did he do? He gave himself a little wink!

I remarked on his optimistic, buoyant spirit. "Do you have to work at that?" I asked. Michael replied, "I just feel that way. I've been so lucky in my life." He calls Parkinson's a "gift"—the "gift that keeps on taking." He's joking, but he's serious. He said, "It woke me up to what was possible in life. Whatever I've lost from having Parkinson's, I've found so much."

I've enjoyed a reputation as a team player, or at least I thought I did. But one day I overheard a bit of conversation I was not meant to overhear. Some colleagues at *Dateline* were discussing a story idea. One of them said, "She'll just say no. Jane always says no."

The truth hurt. I knew they were right. Who knows what story was being discussed? Maybe it was the current "get," a celebrity I didn't want to interview, or a cold call I was loath to make. When I said no, I usually didn't mean "categorically not." After reconsideration, I would often change my mind and say, "Well, okay." Whatever the explanation, this person who "always says no"—I didn't like her much.

These days, nobody comes to me more often with requests like—"Can you do this? Can you go there?"—than Kim Sedmake who is the executive producer of the *Your Life Calling* series. She's not just a colleague but a valued friend. It was hard for me to ignore the pattern of "no, no, no." I wonder if Kim noticed the shift when I started responding to her queries with one word—"Absolutely," "Sure," or "Yep!" I try to be so quick on the trigger that I can't second-guess myself.

Sometimes yes lies just beyond my comfort zone and takes conscious effort, but I think I've begun to rewire my brain.

No invites conflict. More yes means less stress.

Chapter Twenty-eight

Commencement

This is where we part company. I have many other stories to share, but you need to get on with your life. This is a beginning. A commencement.

Commencements are usually exercises in delayed gratification. They make you wait to hear your name called, but I regret to say I did not attend my own graduation ceremony. (Like, I had something *better* to do?) My diploma arrived unceremoniously in the mail. But I've made up for it. I've heard "Pomp and Circumstance" for other people many times and even processed in cap and gown as an honoree or a commencement speaker, most notably at my beloved alma mater, Indiana University. One particular occasion stands out because at an electrifying (for me) moment, I became aware that the seven hundred young, upturned faces seemed actually to be listening. Not that anyone but me would remember what I said to the Providence College class of 1995:

When you leave Providence, today or tomorrow, each of you will be leaving something of yourselves behind. I'm talking about the trash you left out. If it's not too late, don't throw that stuff away. Save the poster that hung in your room this semester. Your favorite CDs. A T-shirt. A baseball cap. Term papers—of course—but better yet notes written in your own hand.

If greatness awaits you these handwritten pages will be worth a lot of money to your progeny. If not, you'll treasure them one day—these communications across time and space with yourself.

And don't be too "cool" to pose for those pictures today in your caps and gowns with friends and family. But also take a picture of your room. Your closet. Your desk. Your roommate's unmade bed. Your roommate in the unmade bed. Collect these memories today. These icons of who you are now will one day be the benchmarks of who you were.

I believe in the future, but we live in the now. The sum and total of where we've been propels us forward, but the wise traveler looks back.

Elizabeth Crook is an author and expert on reinvention. She says, "Looking back on life is like seeing a movie for the second time. You notice things that you didn't see the first time; you can see how this led up to that part of the story. And we don't generally do that as we're living our lives. But when we look back, we can see things that were there all along." Elizabeth and I talked about Gid Pool. What she saw was a person who was unafraid of taking risks. And I saw *someone who tries*.

The last commencement address I delivered was to the class of 2010 at the University of Indianapolis, where I took the opportunity to inspire the graduates with some thoughts on failure. J. K. Rowling had gone that route successfully at Harvard, where she'd said, "It is impossible to live without failing at something, unless you live so cautiously that you might as well not have lived at all."

By the way, did you know that *Harry Potter and the Sorcerer's Stone*, the most successful book ever written (after the Bible), had been rejected by publishers at least nine times before finding a home? Rowling said, "That's why successful people in every field are almost universally members of a certain set—the people who don't give up."

In my remarks, I borrowed a line from the greatest orator of the twentieth century, Dr. Martin Luther King Jr., to make my own case for *trying*. "Faith," he said, "is taking the first step even when you can't see the whole staircase."

I exhorted my audience, "Just take that first step." I wasn't talking only to the graduates but to their parents and grandparents—who seemed to be listening.

At the time, we were still in the grip of the Great Recession. "These are trying times. Perhaps you face the future with anticipation and maybe a little anxiety. But have confidence even in what you cannot see . . . There's never been a better time to try."

Life is a process of trial and error. First steps may be missteps. A successful career path can be one step forward and two back. Success is rarely found lying in the open; it takes some groping around in the dark.

My youngest son was a member of the class of 2009. His commencement was held on a fine spring day after the financial crash in the fall of 2008, in case you have to be reminded. Commencement speakers that year had to struggle to find something upbeat to say. Imagine you were among the law graduates looking to your commencement speaker, Ben Bernanke, the chairman of the Federal Reserve, for an upbeat word. This is what they got: "My advice to you is to stay optimistic. Things usually have a way of working out."

Elsewhere that spring, another speaker quoted a modern French philosopher who said, "The trouble with our times is that the future isn't what it used to be." But as I see it, the trouble with the future is if we're too focused on worst-case scenarios we may not be preparing for the best.

I saw a story in the newspaper that I've shared many times. The setting was a night school classroom at a community college. The students included a couple of single mothers, a bus driver, and a security guard. It was a social studies class, and the lesson involved Abraham Maslow's hierarchy of human needs, from bottom to top—physiological, safety, love and belonging, esteem, and self-actualization.

One of the students said, "I work at a shelter, and I think what I do is help people move up the levels."

The professor said a lot of nonprofits try to lift people from the level of mere safety to self-actualization. The discussion inspired a woman in the front row to raise her hand with a question. "What do you call a person who maybe things don't come easy to, but goes to school anyway and wants to move up the levels?"

The professor's reply was inspired. He said, "You would call that person someone who tries."

Albert Einstein, the smartest man of the twentieth century, is hailed for his theory of relativity, which as a political science major I can't begin to explain, though I understand it had to do with the relationship between time and space. But Einstein had a sense of humor and, although I can't verify it, is said to have offered this alternate theory of time: "Time stands still in childhood, breaks into a jog in adolescence, and flies like a bat out of hell after middle age."

Whether or not Einstein said it, there's an error in the equation, at least when it comes to the twenty-first century. It doesn't factor in the long middle age our generation is experiencing.

In the twenty-first century, it's as if time has stretched out. There was a survey in recent years asking baby boomers to identify the number at which *old* age begins. When my fellow baby boomers named a number that actually exceeded our average life expectancy, my husband, the humorist, quipped: "Death is the new old age." But a lot of us are going to exceed the average life expectancy, and I fervently hope the joke's on him and that Garry is one of them.

Garry's forty-three-year run on the comics page with *Doonesbury* belies his incredibly varied career interests. Broadway. Off Broadway. TV. Magazine essayist. He's known both failure and success, but he's the optimist in the family—always ready to try again.

As Patty Sutherland said of her Tuscany reinvention, "You're not quite sure how it's going to work out, but you still want to try something new. I mean it gets your adrenaline going, it keeps you alive."

We are not the Greatest Generation, but we aren't merely the biggest generation either. I think we're going to be "the luckiest generation" because we're the reinvention generation. We've been given a second chance—to do the thing we'd always wanted to do, or never had a chance before to do, or never imagined we could. I think of these as our "trying times," a time to try new things, and maybe even a time to try *big* things. Maybe we'll confound everyone and redeem our youthful promise yet. As Tony Tata put it, "We're facing some challenges in this country. If we don't cowboy up, who will?"

• • •

I set up a home office, and when I walk in the door, the first thing I see is a big picture of myself. It's not a monument to my ego. It's a poster from *The Jane Pauley Show*. The younger woman in that picture inspires me—because she was "someone who tried." Going forward in life—whether I'm reaching for a new opportunity or adapting to some unforeseen contingency—*this* is how I will define success: being *someone who tries*.

I expect to be cycling in and out of reinvention for the rest of my healthy life. I believe that you never stop growing until you stop trying.

In journalism school, you're taught not to "bury the lead." But as I didn't attend journalism school, I'll put the headline here at the bottom. *Inspiration Is Everywhere, but You Have to Be Looking.* And I hope you find it—everywhere you look!

Acknowledgments

I have often said that the secret to reinvention is that there isn't one. And it's no secret that I didn't make this book happen all by myself. Thank you, Catherine Whitney. You are behind every line.

I am especially grateful to my longtime friend and agent, Wayne Kabak, who has been a wise and supportive voice through many decades and many endeavors. Wayne urged me to write this book and helped find the perfect home in Simon & Schuster. Jon Karp's enthusiasm for the project was heartening to me, and my editor Priscilla Painton has managed a perfect blend of being supportive while allowing me the freedom to write. She embraced the reinvention theme from the start and has been masterful in helping bring this book into being. Thanks, too, to associate editor Sydney Tanigawa, for invaluable support. And I couldn't have done it without Lisa Goins, my intrepid assistant.

The inspiration for this book was the series I developed in partnership with AARP and *Today*. AARP has been a generous and innovative partner. *Today* will always be home to me. Thanks to the whole family—current and former. Special thanks to Matt Lauer. And to Jim Bell, who was supportive from the first pitch. His offhand remark that *Your Life Calling* was "Jane's wheelhouse" was as validating for me as the awards the series has won.

Particular credit for those awards goes to the AARP production team I've had the privilege of working with since 2010. Our team has grown! I wish I had space to personally thank every person who has been involved in this effort. You know you have my gratitude. Special appreciation and affection go to Kim Sedmak, whose title Executive Producer doesn't encompass the multiplicity of roles she plays in the series, and in my life. Thank you, Kim, for being imaginative, tireless, and devoted to the mission. And to my writing partner Peter Nissen, thank you for being a night person. We've been a great team.

I want to thank my travel companions. As my husband put it, we really are "seeing the country" together. You guys are the best: Chief Videographer Borden McKinnon; Director of Photography George Sozio; Chief Sound Recordist Ted Roth; Lighting Director Bob Lloyd.

And back at the ranch: Production Manager Simon van Steyn; Research Manager Robin Cochran; Editorial Producer Barry Yeoman; Segment Producers: Ed Baxter, Lauren Cardillo, Mike Sobola, Graziella Steele, and Deb Long; Senior AARP Broadcast Post-Production Supervisors: Robert Martindale and Nicolas Gouffray; Graphics Team Karen Kim, Alix Léger, and

Osman Malik; Editors: Kevin Lanigan, Scott Newman, Patricia Abeo, Tanya Spann Roche, Melanie Maholick, Steve Fine, and Don Fish; Voiceovers: Karen Ryan.

My affection, admiration, and gratitude to Production Manager Simon van Steyn and Web Writer and Promotions Coordinator Connor Toomy are only exceeded by my confidence in your bright futures. I hope you'll remember how much fun we had and how much you learned at www.lifereimagined.org /janepauley.

Thank you, Mario Diab, Gregg Hubbard, and Barbara Stone, for giving me the star treatment. To make television without you would be unimaginable.

Of course, at the heart of the reinvention stories are the remarkable men and women who have always taught me something new and inspired me in unexpected ways. I am so glad to be able to introduce them to readers: Paul Giannone, Betsy McCarthy, Gid Pool, Jerry Leener, Jan Erickson, the Giacomini family (Bob and his daughters, Diane, Karen, Lynn, and Jill), Tony Tata, Kirk Rademaker, Richard Rittmaster, Sue Halpern, Catherine Silverman, Tripp Hanson, Thomas Betts, Antoinette Little, Mary Reed, Jenny Bowen, Ken Wood, Joe Liles, Orlando Ward, Trudy Lundgren, Lawrence McRae, Michael Allen, Lauren Walters, Barbara Chandler Allen, Sylvia Abrego-Araiza, Catherine Zimmerman, Barbara O'Grady, Bill and Patty Sutherland, and Dawn Nakamura Kessler. If I'm lucky, there will be a sequel, because there are many other people I'd like readers to know. Thank you all for showing us the aspirational side of life. Please keep in touch. Thank you, Kirk, for your recent email: "Funny, although I'm an optimist and constantly visualize success, one of my nagging thoughts is, 'Well yeah, that was it, I've crested and it's gonna be a long, steady coast downwards.' I am delighted to report—no way. I just got back from Switzerland. . . ."

In my years-long exploration of reinvention, I have appreciated the insights and expertise of genuine experts, some of whom I count now as friends, including Marc Freedman, Marci Alboher, Elizabeth Crook, Elizabeth Craig, and Betsy Werley. Also Richard Luker, who has made contributions on both sides of the fence—as expert guide and subject. I'm deeply grateful to Professor Herminia Ibarra; though I've only known her through books and articles, she has taught me to think differently. And Linda Carstenson is doing more to help people see the future in powerful and positive new ways than I can even imagine. I'm grateful to have accidentally discovered Cary Tennis on the web.

A key aspect of my personal reinvention has been mental health advocacy. Thanks to Patrick and Lore McGovern for creating the research community, which daily is pushing the boundaries and changing lives for the better at the McGovern Institute for Brain Research at MIT. And to Bob Desimone, the director, for letting me feel part of it. And thanks to my colleagues on the Leadership Advisory Board for the privilege of having such colleagues!

Kudos to me for choosing wonderful friends. This is far from a complete list. But for letting me share your stories, thanks and love to Ann Kolbell, Meg Hirschfeld, Belinda Broido and Jeffrey Weingarten, Katy Dobbs, Judy Abbett, and Roger Rosenblatt. Thanks for great stories and good times and friendship—Eric Kolbell, Jon Abbett, Fred Newman, and John Hirschfeld. Thank you to all the Uncommon Readers, and especially to Ginny Rosenblatt for founding our book club and inviting me to join it. Thank you, Robin Sanders, Erin Moriarity, Jackie Leo, Janelle Procope, and Carrie Harmon, for your inspiration both personal and practical.

I must acknowledge my beloved "island girls" and the "roomies" who have shared each other's adventures and reinventions under many summer moons.

And burying the lead again, thank you to my beloved family. Of course, I will be forever looking up to my big sister, Ann.

And as I wrote *Your Life Calling: Reimagining the Rest of Your Life*, my children were each in active reinvention modes. Rickie, Ross, Tom (and Juli!), I love and admire you so deeply. You inspire me to keep trying.

Finally, acknowledging the obvious, life without my husband, Garry, would be unimaginable.

About Jane Pauley

O ne of America's most respected broadcast journalists, Jane Pauley has been a familiar face on morning, daytime, and primetime television. She was the co-host of *Today* from 1976 to 1989, anchored *Dateline NBC* for eleven years, and hosted her own daytime program, *The Jane Pauley Show.* In 2004, Pauley published her memoir, *Skywriting: A Life Out of the Blue* (Random House), which became a *New York Times* bestseller. Pauley created the award-winning series *Life Reimagined Today*, produced in collaboration with AARP, which has appeared on *Today* since 2010.

Pauley has received numerous Emmy Awards and has been honored by the Radio and Television News Directors Association (RTNDA) for lifetime contribution to electronic journalism and for Outstanding Achievement by an Individual by American Women in Radio and Television (AWRT). A winner of the prestigious Walter Cronkite Award for Excellence in Journalism, she was inducted into the Broadcasting and Cable Hall of Fame in 1998.

Pauley is a longtime advocate for children's health and education. The National Alliance on Mental Illness (NAMI) presented her with its highest honor, the Rana and Ken Purdy Award.

Pauley and her husband, *Doonesbury* cartoonist Garry Trudeau, are the parents of three grown children.

Orlando Ward

Sue Halpern

Antoinette Little

Anthony Tata

Tripp Hanson

MO

HEALTH CLIN

SPONSORED
BY
MCRAE PROSTA
AWARENESS F
334 226 1177

Trudy Lundgren

Ken Wood